TEACHING SOCIAL WORK PRACTICE

TEACHING SOCIAL WORK PRACTICE

A programme of exercises and activities
towards the Practice Teaching Award

MARK DOEL

Steven Shardlow
Catherine Sawdon
David Sawdon

Published by
Arena
Ashgate Publishing Limited
Gower House
Croft Road
Aldershot
Hants GU11 3HR
England

Ashgate Publishing Company
Old Post Road
Brookfield
Vermont 05036
USA

British Library Cataloguing in Publication Data

Doel, Mark
 Teaching Social Work Practice: Programme of Exercises and
 Activities Towards the Practice Teaching Award
 I. Title
 361.307

Library of Congress Catalog Card Number: 95–81148

ISBN 1 85742 327 5

Typeset in Palatino by Raven Typesetters, New Crane Street, Chester and printed in Great Britain at the University Press, Cambridge.

Contents

Preface and acknowledgements

This book has grown out of the curriculum for the Practice Teaching Award, developed by the Joint Centre for Training and Development in the Personal Social Services. The Joint Centre was a collaborative venture, bringing together social work agencies and education establishments in south Yorkshire, north-east Derbyshire and north Nottinghamshire. The training programme continues as a collaborative venture in its new location at the University of Sheffield, where it is offered as a Diploma/MA in Practice Teaching.

The activities and exercises in *Teaching Social Work Practice* have been developed over a number of years, and we have been in the privileged position to try and test them with hundreds of practitioners who trained to become practice teachers. This book is the fruit of all our work – trainers and participants.

In particular, we would like to record thanks to Dave Henry, who has brought fresh perspectives and much-valued diversity to the teaching team. Thanks are also due to Yvonne Channer and Philip Proctor for their contributions as, respectively, present and past members of the team, which continues to expand. We would also like to thank Janet Atkinson; as Coordinator of the Joint Centre until 1994, she gave unfailing support and commitment to this project.

It is also important to record our thanks to all the practice teachers on the taught programmes, who have given such useful feedback about these activities and helped to re-shape them, and to the practice tutors (sometimes known as mentors or practice assessors), whose experience and reflections have been a significant factor in the development of the course and this book.

Introduction

This book is written with two purposes in mind. The first is to help practitioners to become practice teachers. Each chapter covers a particular aspect of practice teaching, with groups of three chapters covering a larger theme. These are designed to give a comprehensive introduction to the teaching of social work practice.

The second purpose is to assist the reader to study for the Practice Teaching Award. Each chapter in the book gives suggestions about how you might collect evidence of your practice teaching skills and present them in a portfolio. In summary, the book is intended to help you, the reader, to develop your teaching skills and to gather and present evidence of these skills in the form of a portfolio.

The book is not intended solely as a 'how-to-do-it' manual. Certainly, there are tips about how to practice teach, with activities linked to each chapter to help you consider your own practice teaching skills and knowledge. However, manuals tend to tell their readers *the* way to do things, and practice teaching is not that clear-cut. The exercises, activities and notes in this book are designed to develop your skills of self-reflection, so that your practice teaching never becomes the 'right' or 'only' way to do things.

Teaching Social Work Practice is designed to help you to achieve the Practice Teaching Award, but your development as a practice teacher does not end at that point. The book aims to give tools which will help you to continue to evaluate your teaching and to keep your ideas of good-enough practice teaching under regular review.

Open learning

Teaching Social Work Practice has been written in the style of an open learning workbook. This means that you, the reader, should be able to use it independently of trainers or tutors, and at your own pace. The activities and text are intended to be a practical aid to your independent learning.

One of the potential disadvantages of open (or distance) learning is the possibility of feeling isolated and unsupported. For this reason, we hope that the learning can take place in a number of different ways, partly on your own and partly in small support groups. Most of the activities in the book can be carried out independently, but they all benefit considerably from group participation.

Using this book

Although the chapters are tidily numbered from 1 to 22, there is only a loose sense of chronology in this book. It is important to be aware of the whole before you embark on parts of it, and themes which are highlighted in a certain module (such as anti-oppressive practice teaching in Module 3) are also threaded throughout. Taking a piece of music as an analogy, each note follows the previous note in chronological order, but successful musicians have to be aware of the whole piece if they are to bring rhythm and consistency to the performance. Similarly, with the development of practice teaching skills, it is necessary both to focus on individual areas of learning, but also to gain an understanding of how they fit together to form a whole.

Issues such as assessment of the student's ability, which are the focus of Module 7 in this book, cannot be left until the end in practice. Developing a fair climate for assessment (Chapter 19) and groundrules for the way the student will be assessed (Chapter 20), and even what will happen if you judge that the student is not yet ready to practise (Chapter 21), are all factors you need to consider *before* the placement begins.

It will be an advantage to have worked through the book before a student starts the placement, so that you are familiar with the issues and you have done some preparatory work. However, this will be a luxury for some, who will have to learn while running the placement itself.

Introduction to the chapters

Each chapter is accompanied by an activity, to trigger your thinking and understanding of the relevant issues. This activity is intended to be fun, and usually benefits from small groupwork, so try to make sure that you are part of a support network of other practitioners using the book. Some guidance about how to use the activity and the purpose of the chapter is given at the beginning of each chapter. This is followed by the activity itself, and then by a set of notes.

The *Notes for practice teachers* in each chapter provide background to its subject. They may provide a digest of some of the writings about the subject, with pointers to texts you could follow up. The notes sometimes outline a model which you could put into practice in your own teaching, or they may elaborate on the issues raised by the activity. The general intention of the notes is to help your understanding about the subject of the chapter, and to guide your practice teaching. They can be used alone or as a focus for discussion in small practice teacher groups. The references to texts are suggestions if you are interested in pursuing certain themes.

At the conclusion of each chapter, there are suggestions about the way the particular area of practice teaching can be presented in a *practice teaching portfolio*. These are illustrations, not stipulations, and you should not feel that you have to follow the example in the box. They are intended to give you an idea of good practice and the kind of evidence which the assessors of your portfolio will be looking for. Of course, it is important that you are familiar with the requirements of the practice teaching programme with which you have enrolled. Chapter 22 focuses specifically on the portfolio, with some handy hints on putting one together.

Introduction to the modules

The requirements for the Practice Teaching Award are set out by CCETSW (1991b) in Paper 26.3 (see page 190), revised in Paper 26.4. The seven modules of this book (each composed of three chapters) are based on the way CCETSW's requirements have been interpreted by one particular Practice Teaching programme (South Yorkshire). These requirements are presently under review, but it is likely that the content of the Practice Teaching Award will include the seven broad areas which provide the framework for this book.

Module 1, **Context of Practice Teaching**, concerns developments in the way students learn social work practice, from models of student supervision to models of practice teaching. This module explores the value of prior learning and how to make use of it, and the value of involving other people in the process of mapping your practice teaching skills.

Module 2, **Organization of the Placement**, looks at the working parts of a placement: a placement profile as general publicity about what is on offer; the Learning Agreement to frame the individual student's placement, and the preparation around beginnings and endings of placements.

Module 3, **Anti-oppressive Practice Teaching**, explores power in the practice teacher–student relationship, and an understanding of the impact of personal biography on the central issues in practice teaching. This module looks specifically at anti-racist practice teaching, as well as developments in the notion of cultural competence.

Module 4, **Models of Learning**, focuses on adults as learners. It develops abilities in the essential skills of giving and receiving feedback, and reviews the significance of the different learning styles of adults and the need to respond to these. This module also looks at the factors which can block students' learning.

Module 5, **Content of Practice Teaching**, outlines developments in the practice curriculum, especially the idea of modular learning and the way in which CCETSW's requirements for the Diploma in Social Work can be put into practice. This module also looks at the question of how practice teachers can help students to integrate theory and practice.

Module 6, **Methods of Practice Teaching**, introduces the wide range of methods, or Action Techniques, available to the practice learner. It gives guidance about planning and using the practice tutorial, or student supervision session, and about designing and using activities for learning. There is a model for direct observation of the student's practice and hints about the use of video.

Module 7, **Examination of Ability**, concerns the structures and processes used to assess the student's practice competence. The importance of a fair assessment climate and the systematic collection of evidence are highlighted. This module also details the notion of *readiness to practise* and the factors to consider when a student is on the margins of competence.

The final section deals with **The Portfolio**, with practical advice about how to put a portfolio together. The Bibliography contains references for the literature mentioned in the text, and finally, there is a list of suggested core texts to follow up for each area of practice teaching.

Module 1

Context of Practice Teaching

1 Models of practice teaching

About Activity 1   To supervise or to practice teach?

To supervise or to practice teach? is an introduction to four different models of teaching social work practice. Of course, there are overlaps between each of the four models, but they are presented as a start to thinking about your own experiences as a learner of practice. In general, this book uses the structured learning approach, while not discarding the best of the other models.

Purpose

To gain an understanding of different approaches to teaching and learning social work practice, and familiarity with some of the changes in practice learning over recent years. These changes mean that your own experience of learning practice might be different from current expectations of the role of the practice teacher.

Method

- Consider how the four models presented in *To supervise or to practice teach?* relate to your own experiences as a practice learner.
- What do you think are the advantages and disadvantages of each of the approaches?
- Thinking of your present interest in practice teaching, what approach most attracts you?

Variations

You might find it helpful to look at *Activity 1* on your own and then in a small group of other practice teachers, to broaden the discussion. Don't forget to keep some notes for your portfolio about these issues.

Activity 1   To supervise or to practice teach?

Growth and development

- largely individual teaching
- emphasis on student's feelings
- development of self-awareness
- reflective style of supervision
- premium on confidentiality

Philosophy

- *therapeutic models*
- *professional performance depends on personal growth*
- *psychological theories*
- *emphasis on process*

Structured learning

- a planned curriculum, often in modular form
- systematic and varied teaching methods
- use of simulations
- pre-defined standards for assessment
- team teaching common

Philosophy

- *educational models*
- *direct observation important*
- *adult learning theories*
- *outcome and process in balance*

Apprenticeship

- primary relationship with supervisor
- work with available cases
- global, *ad hoc* approach
- supervision as discussion, use of process records
- rate of progress measured

Philosophy

- *learning by doing*
- *good practice means replicating existing work practices*
- *behavioural theories*
- *process and outcome in balance*

Managerial

- planned workload
- skills-based
- problem-solving approach in supervision
- success measured as ability to follow procedures
- emphasis on agency policy as arbiter of good practice

Philosophy

- *learning by doing*
- *protection of clients paramount*
- *rule-directed behaviour*
- *emphasis on outcome*

Thinking back to your own student days, what were your own experiences of supervision and practice teaching, in relation to these four approaches?

- What do you think are the advantages and disadvantages of each of these approaches?
- Where would you locate your own approach to practice teaching, and where would you *like* to locate your approach to practice teaching?

Notes for practice teachers

There have been many changes in the way students are expected to learn the practice of social work. It is important to become acquainted with these changes because expectations are likely to be different from the way in which you experienced your own learning. You will need to consider carefully whether practice teaching is something you can and want to do.

The change of terminology from 'student supervision' to 'practice teaching' reflects a change in emphasis and style. Whereas student supervision has generally drawn more from theories of therapeutic involvement, practice teaching is developing more from theories of learning, with an emphasis on curriculum development.

This book uses a framework derived from the structured learning model described in *Activity 1*. It will help you to develop a planned curriculum, with a systematic use of various teaching methods and agreed criteria for assessment; at its heart is an emphasis on both you and your student as adult learners.

Other authors have identified different categories to describe models or approaches to practice teaching. For example, Bogo and Vayda (1987) identify these six approaches to 'field instruction' (the North American term for practice teaching):

- apprenticeship model
- growth-therapeutic approach
- role systems approach
- academic approach
- articulated approach
- competency-based approach

Yet another way to draw categories is to think of the different *functions* of practice teaching – for example, educative/learning, supportive/helping and administrative/managing (Butler and Elliott, 1985: 14).

In pinning our colours to the mast of structured learning, it is important not to lose sight of the valuable elements which are found in the other three models of practice outlined in *Activity 1*. The individualized nature of the growth and development model, the hands-on directness of apprenticeship, and the accountability to the people who use the service in the managerial model are all factors which can be incorporated into the structured learning approach. It is also necessary to be aware of the possible dangers of this approach; relegating an individual student's needs to the demands of a curriculum, fragmenting the student's experience, etc. These pitfalls can be avoided, but only if their potential is acknowledged.

To supervise or to practice teach? is an opportunity for you to reflect on your past experiences and current practices. You may not have been conscious of using a particular model of learning or teaching social work practice, but when you review the four models as briefly described, some aspects will feel more familiar than others. Where would you locate your own approach to practice teaching? Bogo and Vayda (1987: 1) describe the practice teacher as needing 'to learn to travel a new road between the [college] system and the service provider'. Is that how it feels for you?

Expand the factors and philosophies which underpin each of the four models. Picture four placements in your agency, each one offering a different model of practice teaching. What do you think would be the practical differences for each of the four students in these placements?

Finding 'a good fit'

One factor which it is useful to consider is how the model for teaching and learning should reflect the kind of learning which is to take place. This might be described as 'congruency'; in other words, is there a good fit between the approach to teaching and the purposes for which the learning is taking place?

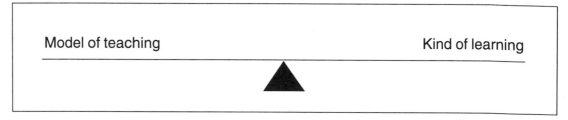

For example, using the four types of models described in *Activity 1*, what approach do you think would be most appropriate in these circumstances, and why?

- to work a till as a cashier at the local supermarket
- to treat patients as a doctor in a general practice
- to fly an aeroplane as a pilot for an airline
- to represent constituents as a Member of Parliament
- to sell life insurance as a salesperson
- to train for the bar as a lawyer
- to help people as a counsellor for Relate

What model of teaching do you think fits best with the work you do?

Links with other chapters

There is further discussion of the differences between traditional approaches to supervision and more recent developments in practice teaching in Chapter 16 (see pages 130–33 in particular).

A theory of practice teaching, developed by Bogo and Vayda (1987), is described in Chapter 15 (page 121).

The concept of congruency is developed further in Chapter 19 (pages 157–8), in relation to the 'fit' between methods of assessment and the student's learning.

Every chapter in this book (including the structure of the book itself) provides examples of the structured learning approach.

The practice teaching portfolio

Record your thoughts about the activity *To supervise or to practice teach?* and reflect on your own approach to practice teaching. It will be interesting to return to these reflections after you have supervised a student on placement, to see how these initial thoughts have changed.

Example 1

Mussaret was about to take her first student on placement and she was attracted to the structured learning approach to practice teaching. As a student, she had had an unhappy experience of 'uninvited therapy', which made her wary of the growth and development approach. However, in listing the pros and cons of each model, she had decided not to throw the baby out with the bathwater, and to incorporate some of the best features of the growth and development approach alongside the structured learning model.

Using a specific example from a practice teaching session with her student, Mussaret briefly described in her portfolio how she made use of these two approaches, helping the student to develop self-awareness by using a structured activity. She made a brief note of what worked well from the student's point of view, and what she would do differently next time.

Further guidance about how to develop your practice teaching portfolio is available in Chapter 22.

2   Prior learning

About Activity 2   Previous experiences

Previous experiences is a collection of questions to trigger discussion about prior experiences. These triggers can be used to explore your own prior learning or your students', or both together.

Purpose

The purpose of this chapter is to focus on the values, knowledge and skills which underpin your practice teaching. This is also reflected in the way you are able to show your value for the experiences and prior learning which your student brings to the placement. The chapter also focuses on your attitude to 'mistakes' and offers a way of framing social work practice (the 'practice compass', page 12).

Method

Consider the seven areas outlined in the *Previous experiences* activity. You may want to add or substitute some others. You can use these questions to trigger discussion with yourself, or as a starter for opening up these issues with a student.

   Either way, keep some notes about your reflections to help you compile this part of your portfolio.

Variations

In common with many of the activities in this book, you will probably find it helpful at some stage to check your ideas and notes with other practice teachers. In particular, it can be fruitful to discuss the seven areas in a small group of four to six practice teachers and students.

Activity 2   Previous experiences

Students come to the placement with a unique constellation of experiences. It is important to value these experiences and to relate them to the learning opportunities on placement.

Use these headings to make links between prior experiences and present learning. Ask for specific illustrations rather than generalized comments, and be sure the students understand that you respect their right to disclose as much or as little as they wish.

Experiences of learning and teaching

What skill has the student recently learnt (e.g. abseiling, using a word processor, speaking a foreign language)? How did she respond to being a learner? Has she ever been 'teacher'? (She might interpret this broadly – e.g. to include some aspects of parenting.) How did she respond to the teaching role?

Experiences of risk-taking and challenge

Is the student cautious by nature, or does he throw himself into things? For example, how would he enter an unheated outdoor swimming pool (a plunging dive? step by step? not at all!)? What is the largest risk which the student feels he has taken in the last few years? How has he responded to a specific challenge in the last year or so?

Experiences of difference and diversity

How regularly does the student experience difference and diversity, and in what ways? What is her response – do these experiences leave her feeling relatively powerful or powerless? Ask her to describe particular instances (e.g. as a young, able-bodied female volunteer at a lunch club for older, disabled men; as a black leader of an all-white choir).

Experiences of trauma and crisis

Has the student experienced a crisis in recent times (his own or somebody else's?)? How does he think he responded? Again, make sure the student feels OK about the level of disclosure; it is preferable to look for a crisis or trauma which resulted in a positive learning experience (even though the outcome may have been 'a failure', he may still feel to have learnt positively from it).

Experiences of success and failure

What kind of success does the student feel she has had in recent times, and how does she respond to positive strokes? How does the student respond to failure, and – taking an actual incident – how has she actually responded (discouragement? blame? try again?)? How does she view the gap between her ideal and actual self?

Experiences of organizing time and priorities

When did the student last feel pressurized, and how did he react? What kinds of pressures does he cope with best, and which ones tend to 'throw' him? Does he see himself as a relatively organized or disorganized person, and how does he think other people see him?

Experiences of teams and groups

What teams and groups is the student involved in (sports, social, etc.)? When does she like to be independent, and when does she enjoy working with others?

Notes for practice teachers

As a practice teacher, you need to consider how you will introduce the items outlined in the *Previous experiences* activity, and whether there are any other areas you would like to add. Will you open up a discussion in which you, too, share your experiences? Remember that this is primarily the student's time, and that your concern is to value their prior learning; it might be rather early at this stage to make connections with the kind of work they will be doing on the placement, but it is helpful to let the student know that you will be making these links at various points.

Valuing mistakes

In their *Guide to Student-Centred Learning*, Brandes and Ginnis (1992) make a plea for mistakes to be valued as opportunities for learning. They go even further by suggesting that 'it can be useful to do away with the whole notion of right and wrong anyway ... an ethos of exploration, of lateral thinking of endless possibilities, can be much more productive than a search for correctness' (Brandes and Ginnis, 1992:48).

Clearly, there is a tension between the liberal philosophy of Brandes and Ginnis, which frees students to explore and take risks, and a view of good practice as having certain prescribed elements such as anti-oppressive behaviour. For example, is there a point at which a student's sexist behaviour becomes not just poor practice but 'wrong'? Is it helpful to look at the behaviour in right–wrong terms? These are themes which should be introduced and maintained in your work as a practice teacher.

The student also needs to be aware of the tension between the value placed on mistakes as an opportunity for learning, and the need to demonstrate competency to gain the social work qualification. We will return to this theme in other chapters (notably 18, 19, 20 and 21), but it should be introduced openly at the beginning of your work with the student.

You will, of course, make mistakes in your work as a practice teacher, and the student is likely to learn from the way you respond to these mistakes. As your experience of practice teaching grows, you will be developing your own understanding of what constitutes better and worse practice as a practice teacher. Reflecting on these mistakes and making changes in response to them is an indication that you are developing your practice teaching.

Use the 'practice compass' below to plot a piece of practice. You could focus on an incident from your own practice teaching (e.g. 'the time I criticized the student's court report') or on the student's practice learning (e.g. 'the time the student persuaded the client to accept volunteer help'). Try plotting it along each axis in turn (right–wrong/good–poor), and make a note of how each axis has a different impact on the way you think about the piece of practice.

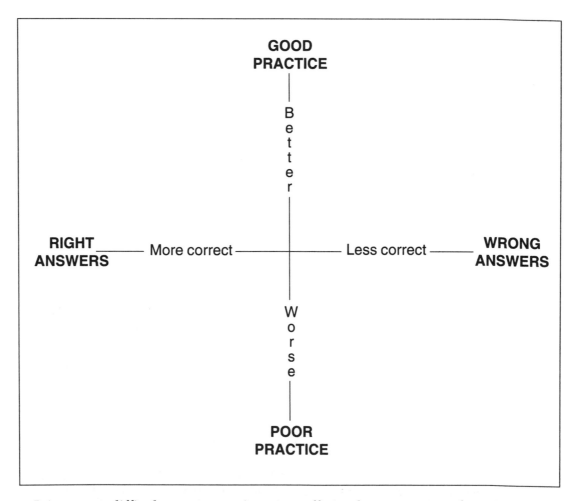

It is not too difficult to see experiences as offering better or worse learning opportunities. However, to what extent can social work practice be considered *right* or *wrong; good* or *poor*?

Your own prior learning

We have been looking at ways to value the student's own prior learning as a basis for her or his work with you. In a similar vein, it is important to think about the way your own previous experiences are going to be of value to your work as a practice teacher. After all, the knowledge, values and skills which you have been using in your work as a social worker are going to be an important base from which to develop your practice teaching.

If you are new to practice teaching, it might be difficult to know at this stage what to highlight. Even so, make a checklist of some attributes which you think are going to be helpful to your development as a practice teacher; you might find it helpful to use the seven areas outlined in the *Previous experiences* activity. It will be interesting to look back at this list after you have completed a placement with a student, when you will be in a better position to add to it.

Values

If you expect your students to be open about their values, you will need to demonstrate this openness, too. Your values do not stand in isolation from your personal biography, so they should be set in the context of your own race, gender, class and generation, etc. Social work practice has its own value base, part of which is a respect for difference and diversity, but which also recognizes the inequality in the power base of these different value systems. In part, to speak of *a* social work value base which values diversity is a paradox: how could you value a set of principles which does not value other principles? And yet – if you are to value difference, how could you not value them?!

It is important to acknowledge and discuss these paradoxes and dilemmas, because they are very much part of the backcloth to social work practice which the student is learning. They are not word-games, but very important ethical issues which lace social work practice all the time.

A concrete way of considering your value base is to consider what you would do in some specific practice teaching situations. Some examples are given below, and you can add to these as real dilemmas occur during the student's placement with you.

- There is a conflict between the student's learning needs and the needs of a client or user of the agency.

- There is a conflict between the student's religious beliefs and a client's wishes.

- There is a conflict between your desire to give and receive honest feedback (including when this is critical) and differences in power and status between you and the student.

- There is a difference between the way your student has handled a situation and the way you would have handled it.

The practice teaching portfolio

Make a note of your responses to the seven areas outlined in the *Previous experiences* activity. If you have the opportunity to use this kind of activity with a student, describe how you approached two or three of these areas, and reflect on how it worked out.

You will be developing a Personal Practice Teaching Profile for your portfolio (Module 4), and as part of this you will need to describe the values which underlie your approach to practice teaching. It is always helpful to illustrate this with a specific example of what you did when one or more of these principles came into conflict. You could relate this conflict to the idea of right–wrong and good practice–bad practice introduced in this chapter.

Example 2

Sean collected examples of practice teaching, as they occurred, which he felt lay in one of the four quarters of the 'practice compass' on page 12. Often, an example would lie in more than one sector – for example, a piece of practice teaching which was *right* in terms of agency procedure but *poor* in terms of professional practice.

In his portfolio, Sean briefly described how he helped Winston, the student, to look at the issues which lay behind the dilemma, and how Winston transferred this learning to another similar situation in his own practice later in the placement. The student would not have made this transfer if he had not learnt about the notion of the 'practice compass' from Sean.

---

3   Involving others

About Activity 3   Triangulations

Triangulations is a way of thinking about who you should involve when gathering and presenting evidence about your practice teaching abilities. A playful map of the practice teaching world is designed to trigger ideas about whose considered opinions you might seek.

Purpose

This activity highlights the need to consider how the views of other people – students and clients, in particular – might be incorporated in your portfolio. It surveys some of the difficulties in gathering and presenting these views fairly, and suggests some ways through these concerns.

Method

Study the map on page 17. Your craft, *Practice Teaching Ability*, is somewhere on the Sea of Practice Teaching. Each landing point represents a possible source of information to you about where your craft lies.
Are there any others you want to add?

- How are you going to take readings from the different sources available to you? When should you take these readings?
- There are a number of perils which you will need to avoid or overcome, like the Rocks of Overwork. Are there any other perils you want to include on the map? What strategies do you have to deal with them?
- Use the map as a metaphor for your plan to seek other people's views about your practice teaching abilities.

Variations

You will probably find it helpful to compare your findings with other practice teachers, and to obtain ideas from each other about how you are going to involve others in giving feedback about your practice teaching.

Check to see if your agency has any pro formas which it uses to monitor feedback from students about placement experiences in the agency. Does this information come back to you?

Activity 3   Triangulations

Locating your practice teaching ability is not easy. How will you take readings from the various landing points, and are there any others you would add? What other perils would you map on the Sea of Practice Teaching and how are you going to avoid them?

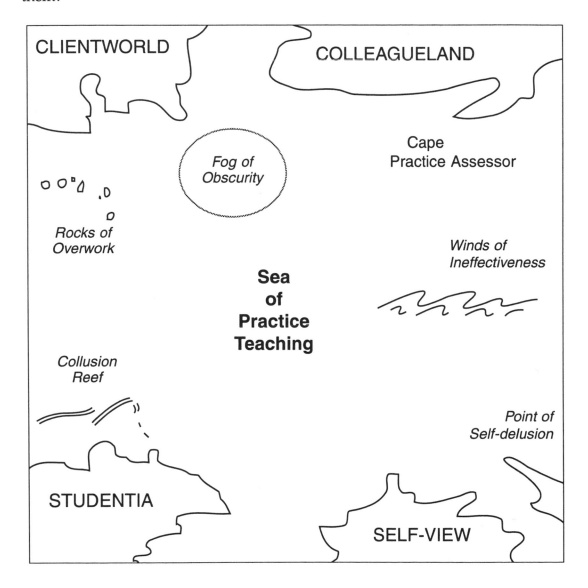

Notes for practice teachers

After you have seen a performance (dance, theatre, concert, sport, etc.) you have a view of what it was like, based on whether you enjoyed it or not and on your expectations of what makes for a 'good' performance. However, if the performers' pay depended on your opinion, you would probably want to take soundings from other people to gain a more rounded picture before you took the responsibility of making a judgement. We might call these people 'reporters': people whose views you wished to be reported. You would also want the reporters to give reasons for their opinions, so you could weigh these against each other.

This process of taking soundings from a number of different sources is called 'triangulating', a nautical term used to plot the position of craft at sea (see Shardlow and Doel, 1993b). The same process should take place when you come to a judgement about a student's abilities, and it should also be apparent when a judgement is being made about your practice teaching abilities. If you were making a list of who should report on your practice teaching, what groups of people would you include?

In general, *students'* views of practice teaching and practice teachers' abilities have not often been sought in a systematic fashion, still less those of *clients*. Unless there is a tradition in your agency of asking for opinions from users about the service in general and your work in particular, attempts to introduce this kind of 'customer feedback' might be viewed as challenging. This would not be the first time that practice teaching has found itself in the vanguard of good practice.

Although the problems involved in seeking views fairly should not be under-estimated, equally they should not be a reason to abandon the attempt. Below, we explore the technical, ethical and personal areas of difficulty, with suggestions for dealing with them.

Technical concerns

Finding out the views of other people is rather like undertaking a small research project (see Doel and Shardlow, 1993: 103–4 and 185–6); as such, it requires time and careful planning.

Students

The practical task of involving students is made easier by the fact that practice teachers usually teach small numbers of students at any one time (and often only one). However, deciding which questions to ask and at what stage in the placement is not so easy. When can the student be expected to make a reasoned judgement about quality?

Early in the placement, students can give their response to issues concerning the climate for learning (see Chapters 10, 11 and 12). Do they feel the learning environment is encouraging, and are there adequate opportunities for learning? Their ability to comment on qualitative aspects of your work will increase as their experience of practice learning develops.

Clients

The technical problems in obtaining the views of clients are much more difficult. There are questions of sampling – it is time-consuming and complex to consider contacting all the clients with whom the student has worked, but difficult to be certain that a sample is representative. (See Chapter 20, page 169, for a discussion of sampling in connection with your assessment of the student's abilities.)

In addition, the client cannot be expected to comment on your practice teaching, since they are one stage removed from this; many factors lie 'in between' your practice teaching abilities and the client's experience of the student's work.

The only questions you can ask with certainty concern the client's experience of the student, which allows you to draw tentative inferences about the quality of your practice teaching. For example, as the teacher of a student dentist, you would want to look at the effectiveness of your customer care teaching if a number of patients described your student's 'drill-side' manner as curt.

Ethical concerns

Students

The relationship between the student and the practice teacher is unequal. No matter how informal and warm it is, the relationship is characterized by a power imbalance, with the practice teacher having the ultimate power to recommend a pass or fail for the student's work. In these circumstances, it is difficult to ask for and receive honest, untainted feedback. Difficult, but not impossible.

It is an important part of the Learning Agreement that issues of power should be discussed and continue to be discussed (see Chapter 5). Part of this dialogue should include how the practice teacher and the student will give feedback to each other (see Chapter 10). In particular, *rules of play* should be agreed beforehand, so that there is a clear expectation about what is allowed and what is not allowed. Marking out the pitch in this way helps to avoid feelings of unfairness later on and adds to a sense of security.

The timing of feedback is critical. It may be necessary to wait until well after a placement before clear feedback about your practice teaching is available from a student where you have recommended he or she is not ready to practise in many areas: 'I know you were very unhappy about my recommendations, but...', with a number of specific questions aimed at particular aspects of your teaching.

Clients

Similar ethical issues apply to the task of shaping feedback from clients, especially the question of an imbalance of power. People who want services from an agency may feel constrained from giving honest feedback, for fear of losing those services or having something bad happen to them. However, Fisher et al. (1986) found that most parents of children in care were able to make a distinction between the decisions made (which they may or may not have been in agreement with) and the quality of service they received. In general, their view of quality did not depend on their agreement with the decision. It is easy to underestimate people's ability to make these distinctions. The secret seems to be to ask in the right way, at the right time.

Personal concerns

There are objective reasons for the technical and ethical difficulties about involving others in how to define quality in practice teaching. However, you should be honest with yourself about whether you *want* this kind of feedback; this is feedback which is very personal and may not be comfortable. Indeed, if it is to be at all useful, it should cover all aspects of your teaching: positive elements as well as those which you need to change.

Moreover, it can feel personally unfair – for example, if you feel that the pressures of other work or the agency's lukewarm commitment have undermined your ability to give a quality service. In these circumstances, of course, it is all the more important to obtain the evidence needed to harden your case for a better environment to support your practice teaching.

Your actions will show whether you *do* want to broaden the way in which quality in practice teaching is defined, by involving others; the technical and ethical difficulties are there to be surmounted.

Baird (1991) suggests that client views should be incorporated in the assessment of competence for the DipSW; by extension, it seems right that students (as the main 'consumers' of practice teaching) should have their views included in the assessment of competence for the Practice Teaching Award. Baird's research (1991: 33) found a reluctance of practice teachers to cooperate, but Shennan (1995: unpublished) discovered a considerable commitment to involving students in assessing practice teaching, though uncertainty about how to put this into practice.

It is interesting that in Baird's study only 4 out of 227 clients refused to be interviewed, and all four of these clients were allocated to one student.

Example questionnaire for a student and practice teacher to complete and discuss together

This is an example of a questionnaire which both you and the student could complete and discuss (only question 6 is specific to the student). If you think it is unrealistic to expect honest answers from students before the end of the placement, they could be asked to do this retrospectively when the placement is completed.

1   How well do you think the Learning Agreement was set up and reviewed?

2   How do you each evaluate the other's skill in (please circle on the scale 1–5):
    – listening
    – giving information
    – giving feedback

- receiving feedback
- handling conflict
- setting goals
- evaluating work
- anti-oppressive practice
- other?

Poor 1 2 3 4 5 Excellent

3 How well do you think learning opportunities have been provided? (Give examples.)

4 How well do you think the practice tutorial/supervision session has been used? (Give examples.)

5 How well do you think the practice competence has been assessed? (Give examples.)

6 Supposing a student colleague was thinking of coming to this placement, would you advise her or him to come? (Give your reasons.)

Any other comments?

Signed ....

The practice teaching portfolio

In this part of your portfolio you will be describing how you have gathered evidence about your practice teaching abilities, especially with regard to how you have involved other people. This means being honest about the difficulties, too.

You might choose to present the evidence itself in different units of the portfolio (e.g. a commentary from a student in connection with issues of power and oppression included in Chapter 7). Use this chapter to cross-reference, so the assessors of your portfolio can make these connections.

Example 3

Judy decided to use the example questionnaire on page 20 with her student, Maria. She had mentioned the questionnaire as an idea early in the placement, and gave Maria a copy at the mid-placement review in order to ask her if she felt OK about the two of them completing it before the end of the placement. With Maria's agreement, Judy included both questionnaires (hers and Maria's) in her portfolio, with a brief commentary on how she had used them to gain as honest a view as possible from Maria, and how she had responded to the information she received. She also gave Maria an opportunity to revise her questionnaire after the placement was completed, though Maria did not make any subsequent alterations.

Judy cross-referenced to other sources of evidence included elsewhere in her portfolio, with a very brief explanation of how this information had influenced her practice teaching.

Module 2

Organization of the Placement

4 Placement profile

About Activity 4   Brochure

Brochure draws a parallel between choosing a holiday and finding out about a placement. You are encouraged to present brief, jargon-free information for the student. This kind of profile will be useful to any newcomers to your work setting, not just prospective students. The process of completing *Brochure* can help to develop a team approach to the student's placement and to the work of the team in general.

Purpose

This chapter focuses on what goes on before the student arrives on placement. At this point there is no particular student in mind, so you are preparing materials for an imaginary student rather than a specific person. The individual tailoring will come later, when a student with a name approaches you.

Method

- Consider the general issues presented on page 26 and the process described on pages 26–7, before turning to the checklist on page 27.
- Putting the practice profile together, as a kind of 'brochure', is not a one-off activity. You will probably want to write parts of it later, when you are more familiar with the materials in this book and with practice teaching in general.
- You should include a copy of the final version of your Personal Practice Teaching Profile in the portfolio.

Variations

When you have completed a profile, it will need revising from time to time; if you can keep it on a word processor disk, it will not take too much time to update it for each subsequent placement.

Involving team colleagues in writing the brochure can act as a focus for team-building to develop a team view on many issues which are easily neglected.

Activity 4   Brochure

When you are planning a holiday to a new place, you usually want to find out all you can about it, so you won't waste your money. You might ask somebody who has already been there, but it is also an advantage to have written information and to see photographs. The problem with holiday brochures is their tendency to appear 'glossy' – often you cannot trust that they are painting a full picture, and they are not written by people who actually live and work there.

So, when you are writing your own brochure about the placement, you need to think how you would like to present the information in a clear, attractive, 'unglossy' way. Who should be involved in putting it together? Can you start from an existing 'mission statement' of values and purposes, or will you have to invent your own?

There are some example headlines on page 27 to help you write your practice placement profile. Before you use that guide, jot down some of the things you would like to make sure went into a brochure of this kind. Make a few notes about how you want to present this information.

The brochure, or practice placement profile, is not a static document. There may be aspects which you cannot complete at this stage, until you have learned more about practice teaching. There may be other parts which you want to revise as you complete the different chapters in this book. Keep your practice teaching profile to hand, so that you can work on it as you progress through this book.

Notes for practice teachers

Creative approaches to the profile

One of the problems with checklists like the one on page 27 is the tendency to produce a rather dry, wordy response. Is it possible for you to convey the kind of information which is included in that checklist in a more imaginative manner? For example, describing a typical day in the life of your team could address most of the topics on the checklist in a way which makes it more real for a prospective student. Can you create something which falls between the dry bureaucracy of an agency policy document and the glitzy hard-sell of a holiday catalogue?

The purpose of the profile is twofold. First, it should help the student to gain an idea of what a placement with you will be like. Students do not have a good deal of choice, given the current economics of placements, but a placement profile gives a public message that you are willing and able to lay out your particular stall.

Second, the process of writing the profile encourages you to think about these issues. Writing something down for public consumption focuses your mind, and it is a starting point to involve team members and close colleagues in the student placement, making it less of an isolated activity for you (see Chapter 5).

Process

Before your thoughts are tainted by the checklist below, jot down some of the key issues as you see them. You could discuss the notion of a student brochure at a team meeting and ask for colleagues' views about its contents (using a brainstorm and recording this on a flip-chart?).

There is likely to be tension between the desire to be comprehensive and the wish to keep the information brief and easy to read. Try prioritizing your content – what are the 'headlines' you want to stand out, and what could be confined to the small print? Is it more important for the reader to find the information interesting and understandable, or for you to dot every 'i' and cross each 't'?

Get other people to look at a draft before the final version. Ask them to think about the language and what general impressions the profile conveys, as well as the fine details. It is interesting to give it to someone who does not know much about social work and see if they like it; make changes to any parts which this person cannot understand. Do you know any budding cartoonists who could add some graphics to lighten the text? Would photographs be a good addition?

If you also hope that the student will enjoy a placement with you, try to communicate it in the way you present this material, and be honest about shortcomings. Ray Brooks always sold his houses by being devastatingly honest in the advertisements ('no room to swing a cat in the kitchen', etc.). You are not 'selling' a placement – the economics of placements are likely to be in your favour for some time – but you are *presenting* it. Thinking about the presentation is likely to help to clarify the placement itself.

Placement profile – Checklist

Social work practice experience

- *Personal:* a brief description of your qualifying training and subsequent practice experience.
- *Team:* a brief overview of the practice experience of the team as a whole and your role in the team.
- *Agency:* how the team fits into the agency's overall structure and any special features of the agency's work (e.g. involvement in a research project) which you think the student would be interested to know.

Knowledge, values and skills

- *Personal:* your areas of special interest and expertise, including any particular methods you use; your style of working and the core values which underpin your practice.
- *Team:* any features you would like to pick out concerning other team members' interests and the team's working style; do members work together a lot, or is the team more a collection of individuals?

- *Agency:* include any mission statement of the agency's purposes and values.

Practice teaching experience

- *Personal:* your experience as a practice teacher and your main interests in practice teaching; the availability of supervision for a student on placement – and its limitations; the learning opportunities the placement is likely to provide, and your teaching styles and methods.
- *Team:* the team's 'student history' – in other words, do other members of the team supervise students, and are they likely to be actively involved with a student placed with you? The kind of cover available to the student if you are absent, and the accommodation and practical resources available to a student (photocopying, library, etc.).
- *Agency:* the support which the agency gives to practice teaching (e.g. discussion groups for students, workload relief for practice teachers, etc.). Summarize any policy statements the agency has drawn up about practice teaching.

Client groups

- *Personal:* the kinds of circumstances which the people you work with find themselves in; you can bring this alive by a brief profile of one or two typical users of the agency's services.
- *Team:* any special projects in the team which the student would be interested in.
- *Agency:* is your work similar to others' in the agency, or are they working with people in different situations?

Anti-oppressive practice

- *Personal:* your commitment to anti-oppressive practice, and how this might show itself to a student on placement.
- *Team:* the composition of the team and how this does or does not reflect the complexion of the people with whom the team works; the team's development in terms of anti-oppressive practice.
- *Agency:* agency commitment to equal opportunities, and how this shows itself.

Further considerations

If, as is likely, the profile has been written in English, should it be translated into other languages? In bilingual areas (such as Wales, New Zealand, Quebec) translation is likely to be in the front of people's minds, but in areas where English dominates, it is easy to forget that it might be a second language for some students.

How would a visually impaired student access the information? Of course, this kind of consideration will lead you to ask broader questions about how your placement and your agency maintains access to people who do not use English as a first language or who have a physical disability (see Chapter 7). The act of putting a student brochure together is a catalyst for these considerations, as well as providing a very helpful end product for students who are thinking about a placement with you.

If you pool your resources with other practice teachers in the same agency, the writing of some general aspects of the profile could be shared.

Links with other chapters

The practical preparations for the placement are considered in Chapter 6 and the sharing of expectations and preparing a Learning Agreement in Chapter 5.

The practice teaching portfolio

You should include the current version of your Personal Practice Teaching Profile in the portfolio. Include any feedback about the profile from students or colleagues, and make any brief comments you choose about the process of putting your profile together.

Example 4

Yusef is a practice teacher in a Family Centre. He had already completed a profile for a previous student placement, and he wanted to keep it up to date.

When Cathy, the student, had been on placement for some time, Yusef asked how she had found the 'brochure', and whether it reflected what the placement had actually felt like for her. Cathy said the brochure was good as far as it went, but the physical setting of the Centre was such an important part of the 'climate' created for students, workers and users that it would really help to include some photographs. Yusef accepted this idea, and he and Cathy took some photos, choosing some which captured the spirit of the Centre, to include with the profile.

---

5 Agreements

About Activity 5   Expectations

Expectations (1 and 2) is a trigger activity to help you think about the issues which you want to discuss with a prospective student. The activities use a sentence completion technique to open up a number of areas where it is particularly important to make sure your expectations and those of the student are explicit.

Purpose

Once you have been approached by the social work programme to consider a particular student for a placement with you, it is important to make an opportunity for you and the student to share your expectations. It is probably less important to achieve a consensus than to be aware of any differences between you.

Method

- The *Expectations* exercises are designed to be used directly with a student, as a trigger to discussion. For the purposes of your own learning as a practice teacher, you need to make some notes about what you learned from using the *Expectations* activities, and what changes you would make next time.
- Later in the placement, reflect on your notes from this preparatory discussion. Did it anticipate any later developments in your work with the student?

Variations

As your experience of practice teaching increases, you will probably want to add – or substitute – sentences to the *Expectations* exercises. You might also want to devise similar activities to use with the college tutor and with colleagues.

Activity 5   Expectations (1)

The practice teacher

General expectations

One of the things I like most about having a student on placement is . . .

One of the things I find most difficult about having a student on placement is . . .

My previous experiences of teaching students have felt . . .

It is particularly important to me that students . . .

One of the best things which I think students can get out of placements is . . .

Specific expectations for this placement

One of my main hopes for this placement is . . .

One of my main concerns about this placement is . . .

Something I wonder might be an issue for us during the placement is . . .

One area of special consideration for me is . . .

The student

General expectations

One of the things I like most about being a student is . . .

One of the things I dislike most about being a student is . . .

My previous experiences of being a student have felt . . .

It is particularly important to me that teachers . . .

One of the best things which I think students can get out of placements is . . .

Specific expectations for this placement

One of my main hopes for this placement is . . .

One of my main concerns about this placement is . . .

Something I wonder might be an issue for us during the placement is . . .

One area of special consideration for me is . . .

Activity 5   Expectations (2)

The practice teacher

1   I like to have close regard of the student's direct work with users/residents:
early in the placement –

1	2	3	4	5
hardly at all				*most of the time*

late in the placement –

1	2	3	4	5
hardly at all				*most of the time*

2   I expect students to be able to take responsibility for their own work:

1	2	3	4	5
very little				*a lot*

3   I use different teaching methods:

1	2	3	4	5
rarely				*much of the time*

4   I will seek colleagues' opinions about your practice abilities:

1	2	3	4	5
not at all				*very frequently*

The student

1   I expect the practice teacher to see me in direct work with users/residents:
early in the placement –

1	2	3	4	5
hardly at all				*most of the time*

late in the placement –

1	2	3	4	5
hardly at all				*most of the time*

2   I expect to take responsibility for my own work:

1	2	3	4	5
very little				*most of the time*

3   I expect to learn using a variety of methods:

1	2	3	4	5
very few				*very many*

4   I expect you to seek clients' opinions about my practice abilities:

1	2	3	4	5
not at all				*very frequently*

Notes for practice teachers

Sharing expectations

The strength of the placement as an opportunity for learning depends on many factors, and one of the most significant of these is how expectations are shared. This dialogue needs to begin at the first contact. First thoughts often change, so it is important that expectations are aired regularly.

The student's expectations may differ from the practice teacher's. It is ignorance of differences rather than the differences themselves which most jeopardizes a placement. A student who expects a nurturing, cosy, hand-holding experience is in for a rude shock if placed with a challenging practice teacher who gives a great deal of scope for his or her students to make their own mistakes. If these contrasting expectations are known beforehand, it is easier to accommodate them (or, in an ideal world, to consider an alternative placement).

A lack of expectations does not mean compliance. For example, when asked to respond to the *Activity 5* item 'I expect to learn using a variety of methods', a student who has only experienced 'chalk-and-talk' teaching might be unaware of student-centred approaches to learning. The absence of expectations does not necessarily indicate that students are neutral on this subject; it could suggest that they have not thought about it or do not understand it. The two *Expectations* activities give both of you an opportunity to go beyond the simple sentence completion or number score exercises, which act as triggers for further discussion.

A team approach to the practice teaching role

Student supervision has typically been a private affair, reflecting the supervision experience of many practitioners. 'My' student was seen as another layer in the supervision hierarchy.

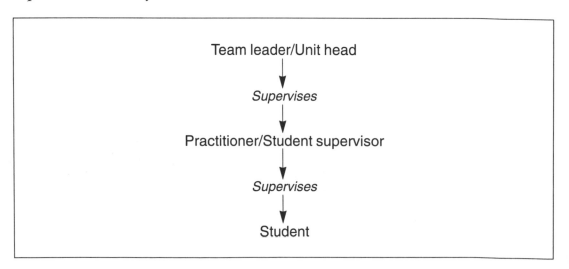

Team leader/Unit head

Supervises

Practitioner/Student supervisor

Supervises

Student

Despite some examples of group supervision and peer review, this line of supervision was characteristic of most students' experience, and it was often remarkably difficult for colleagues to penetrate each separate vertical structure. The sacrosanct supervisor–student relationship tended to discourage sharing, and therefore blocked people from learning from each other's experiences. The student's experience of supervision in most respects emulated the supervisor's (see Gardiner, 1989).

As the supervision role turned towards practice teaching, more explicit styles developed. The curriculum for practice learning has become less implicit, so practice teachers and students can begin to share their experiences, using a common framework. In particular, it became evident that trying to teach the whole curriculum as a one-person band was unrealistic: rather like expecting each class-based teacher to teach the whole range of the class curriculum – socialization, social policy, law, practice methods, research methods, etc. (Doel, 1987b).

The role of the practice teacher is less private, less exclusive. There is more emphasis on the practice teacher's role as a person who organizes appropriate opportunities for the student's learning, not necessarily the person who always 'does' them. You have the responsibility of making sure the learning opportunities are available, but not the responsibility for providing them all.

The implications of this change are considerable. As a practice teacher, you need to think of yourself as having a time-share in the student's placement rather than single occupancy. This will require you to develop teaching packages, so that students do not rely solely on you for their learning. You need to have reliable information about your colleagues' abilities (a team profile) and links with other practice teachers to develop a network of practice seminars. This does not have to be as grand as it sounds; basically, it means that you agree to take a small group of students to look at one particular practice area (e.g. professional boundaries), and the other practice teachers each take other groups along different themes. Once this kind of network has developed, it is not difficult to see how it can save time and also be a better learning experience for the student.

Team teaching

In teams where there are a number of accredited practice teachers, it might be possible to collaborate around the organization, teaching and assessment of a placement. In other circumstances, you may be looking for colleagues to coordinate their activities, so that they do some direct work with the student to help meet some of the learning objectives. As a minimum, you will want their cooperation and agreement to a student placement.

The continuum in the box overleaf is a way of looking at different kinds of involvement. Collaboration may be an ideal to aim for, but it is better not to be too ambitious, and to set realistic expectations. In some teams, cooperation may be the best you can achieve at present.

Cooperation ⟶	Coordination ⟶	Collaboration
Sharing information	*Sharing planning*	*Sharing resources*
People do not hinder each other: (e.g. team members agree that one person can take a student and do not block plans to help that person's aims).	People plan their work to take account of each other's plans: (e.g. there is workload relief for the practice teacher, and team members plan ways to involve the student).	People work closely together (e.g. they all participate in the student's Learning Agreement and share the teaching to help the student achieve different learning objectives).

In summary, team teaching can mean many things. For example:

- joint teaching, where you work together with another practice teacher, who may be in the same work team as you, or in another work team
- a network of teaching, where you and other practice teachers coordinate your efforts
- other colleagues give a student particular hands-on experiences of social work practice, while you do the reflective teaching and the assessment of competence ('long-arm supervision' is based on this model)

Team teaching might not be possible, in which case you will be working as a singleton practice teacher, providing most, and perhaps all, of the opportunities for the student's practice learning yourself. Whatever the arrangements made, it is important that everybody is clear about their roles and that there is an individual, named practice teacher who is coordinating the learning opportunities.

The Learning Agreement

The touchstone for the student's learning is the agreement, or contract. Placement agreements have developed over the last ten years, so they might be different from your own experience as a student if you qualified before this.

The Learning Agreement (sometimes called a 'Placement Contract') comes from the meeting of the individual student, the practice teacher and a representative from the course programme (usually a college tutor) to discuss and record the expectations of the placement. Broadly, this includes the specific learning objectives (the content of the learning), the methods to be used to help the student's learning, arrangements for the assessment of the student's abilities, and any other practical details.

Most programmes have devised their own format for placement agreements. Here are the headings used by the South Yorkshire Consortium for the second placement Learning Agreement:

---

1 names and contacts for the student, practice teacher and tutor
2 student's background, career intentions and learning needs
3 learning opportunities, including work to be undertaken during the placement
4 practice teaching arrangements:
   - who will provide back-up when the practice teacher is unavailable
   - frequency and duration of practice teaching sessions
   - details of others to be involved in teaching modules of the curriculum
   - other support networks available in the agency for the student
5 expected periods of leave during the placement
   - for the student
   - for the practice teacher
6 practical arrangements
   - normal hours the student is expected to work
   - study time
   - workshop dates
   - accommodation available for the student
7 anticipated methods of assessment to be used (tick checklist)
8 signatures of student, practice teacher, agency representative and tutor

---

The development of a more explicit and detailed placement curriculum, sometimes called a 'practicum', has led to comprehensive learning objectives for all students in a particular programme (see Chapters 13, 14, and 15). The individual Learning Agreement is more concerned with how the placement will help the student to achieve these objectives, and the methods to be used to do this.

Workload relief

If it was not apparent before, then the content of this book will certainly have made the extent of the practice teaching task visible. It is vital that you have the time to study for the Practice Teaching Award and to fulfil all your responsibilities as a practice teacher.

CCETSW (1991a: para. 5.2.1) states that approved practice teacher training programmes 'must include an education and training component of a minimum of 150 hours and should normally extend over a period of not less than three months. This component is in addition to the time that a practice teacher training on the programme spends in the supervision of a social work student.' (Candidates with sufficient experience can, of course, submit portfolios to examination boards for the Practice Teaching Award without undertaking this kind of programme.)

Agencies seeking approval for practice learning must demonstrate to CCETSW that they have a commitment to the provision of high-quality practice learning opportunities, which includes 'adjustments to the workloads of staff who undertake practice teaching' (CCETSW, 1991a: para. 2.3.3[c]).

Too often, 'workload relief' means workload *displacement*, as your work is shared out among your team colleagues, and the success of the placement depends on the lubricant of goodwill. Some agencies have taken on staff who work in a peripatetic manner, so that each placement setting gets its fair share of extra help, though not always at exactly the same time as the student is on placement. A few (exceptional) agencies provide extra payment for practice teaching. Some agencies, especially in the voluntary sector, have opened a discussion with teams to see how they might enhance the *quality* of the team's work, if not actually reducing the *quantity* (e.g. one team decided to buy a word processor rather than buy in a few extra hours' staffing).

Whether your agency is relatively well resourced or under-resourced, it is important to get together with other practice teachers to consider ways in which practice learning can progress in the agency. A ginger group can articulate the needs of practice teachers and students, and highlight the agency's responsibilities as a body which is approved for practice learning.

The practice teaching portfolio

Your portfolio should contain a copy of a Learning Agreement you have made with a student you have had placed with you (if this is part of the assessment report, make a cross-reference to it). Was the placement able to fulfil all the expectations of the Learning Agreement? Also, you need to reflect on any team teaching or teaching packages which you have developed with others – how have they worked out in practice?

Example 5

Pat was an experienced practice teacher working in a children and families team in a social services department. She had a very active teaching style, and spent a lot of time in joint work together with her students. On completing the *Expectations* exercise with a prospective student called George, it was clear that he saw himself as a more independent operator.

Nevertheless, Pat and George agreed to go ahead and work with these differences. In reviewing the placement later on, George said that he thought he had benefited from Pat's hands-on style, even though it was very different from what he had experienced before. He was also doing some work with Irene, another member of the team; although this had been done with Pat's knowledge and approval, George had sought this opportunity himself, and Pat admitted to herself that she had felt a bit 'possessive' of her student.

Pat described this briefly in her portfolio, evaluating the impact that the experience had on her practice teaching. She continued to value her active style (and this had been confirmed by George's feedback, too); George's contact and work with another team member had felt threatening at first, but Pat was now alerted to the kind of contribution which other people could make to the student's teaching, and she felt less responsible for all the student's learning. In the end, it had worked out well to have a student whose expectations had been different from hers, but she doubted the result would have been so happy if she had not known about these differences from the beginning.

6 Beginnings and endings

About Activity 6   Bookends

Bookends consists of two checklists to help you to prepare for the start of a student's placement and the end of that placement.

Purpose

There are some aspects of a placement which can be ready for *any* student to start, and there are others which should be tailored to the *particular* student who is about to join you. This chapter helps you consider this preparation.

    Similarly, endings are more successful if they are anticipated. This chapter looks at the significant elements of the endings of placements. Beginnings and endings are gathered into the same chapter of this book because, despite coming at opposite ends of the placement, they are dependent on each other.

Method

- Use the two checklists on pages 40–42 as a trigger to make your own notes to prepare for beginnings and endings.
- Review these checklists after the placement has finished, to see how comprehensive they were.

Variations

You may want to add other categories or headings to the two checklists. Keeping them updated saves time when you are getting ready for the next placement.

Activity 6   Bookends

Think of the process of preparation and the process of ending as two bookends which keep the placement secure.

Checklist for the beginning of the placement

Welcome

Are there any office traditions to welcome a new face?

- Are there flowers on the desk? (OK, it's rare, but it does happen!)
- What introductions are planned?
- What are the lunch arrangements?
- Are team birthdays celebrated?

Where do you go for . . .

- a quiet chat
- a noisy chat
- a pee
- a quiet phone call
- a cup of tea
- lunch
- exercise?

Necessary items

- desk and chair
- telephone
- access to drinks
- access to fresh air
- stationery, diary, pens, identity card
- 'starter' pack of relevant policies and procedures

Boring, but essential

- What are the rules about smoking?
- How do you pay into the tea fund?
- Who should you inform about sick leave?
- What's the deal on personal phone calls?
- Where do you park (and can you claim parking charges)?
- Do you sign in and out?
- What are the fire, health and safety arrangements?

Orientation

- What are the plans for the first few days?
- How are these shared with the student?

Beginnings are not just about what you do and think; they are also about what you feel. How do you generally feel at these beginnings?

- the start of a film
- the beginning of a holiday
- the start of a book
- the beginning of a friendship
- the start of a party
- the dawn
- the start of a cold
- the first day of a new year
- the beginning of something new

How are you feeling about the beginning of the placement?

Checklist for the ending of the placement

The agency's clients

- Ensure the proper closure and write-up of work with clients.
- Ensure the proper continuity of service where this is needed.
- Get feedback from clients about the student's work, where this has been agreed.

The student

- Review the assessment report and any portfolio of student's work.
- Recap the learning which has taken place, helping the student to summarize the current position.
- Return agency 'toys', like the starter pack, identity card, etc., and settle debts, like the tea money!

The next student

- A message from the current student to the next one; what 'tips' would they hand on?

The practice teacher

- Seek feedback from the student about the placement with you.
- Review your notes on how you felt the placement went.

Re-orientation/exit plans

- What's the plan for the last few days? (This should be agreed well in advance.)
- What follows next for the student – college work; a new job; a return to an old job; a search for employment?
- How can you help to prepare the student for this next stage?

Goodbyes

- Are there any office traditions to say farewell (a meal out with the team; a farewell lunch)?
- Are students asked back to the next Christmas 'do'?

Like beginnings, endings are not just about what you do and think; they are also about what you feel. How do you generally feel at these endings?

- the end of a film
- the finish of a holiday
- the end of a book
- the ending of a friendship
- the finish of a party
- the dusk
- the end of a cold
- the last day of the old year
- the end of something familiar
- the end of your tether!

How do you anticipate you will feel about the ending of the placement?

Notes for practice teachers

Beginnings

There are some items which need to be in place ready for any student to walk into, and there are others which will be required by this particular student.

Thinking of students as guests, what should be in general preparation (like a spare bedroom or a fold-away sofa bed for a house guest)? What special preparation should there be for this particular student (like the house guest you know is vegetarian)? Are there any particular networks you need to make available to the student (e.g. a black workers' group to give support to a black student placed in a predominantly white agency)?

Orientation plan

A guided orientation to your agency is a good way of helping the student begin to feel at home. Leaving students to their own devices at this early stage risks them wasting time trying to find their own way around, but you also want to give them some elbow room, so they can begin to find their own pace. A guided introduction is one way of achieving a balance between direction and independence in these first few days (Doel and Shardlow, 1993: 3–12). It sets the tone for the kind of learning which the student will be experiencing during the rest of the placement.

Introducing direct observation

Systematic direct observation of the student's work is a specific requirement for the Diploma in Social Work (CCETSW, 1991b: para. 3.4.4.2). It is also a requirement that your practice teaching will be 'directly and systematically observed' for the Practice Teaching Award, so you are not asking the student to experience anything that you will not undergo yourself (CCETSW, 1991a: para. 5.2.2.b).

In addition to sound educational reasons, there is an obvious need to observe practice as part of the assessment process. In some settings, direct observation of how other people work with the users of the service is an everyday occurrence, impossible to avoid. In other settings, workers do not commonly see other team members in direct contact with the agency's clients, and there is no tradition of observation.

Where the team is unfamiliar or unsympathetic with this approach, it is especially important to plan a careful introduction to direct observation, and it is always best to start this process from the outset.

Together with the student, you should discuss the purpose and process of direct observation. Students will vary in their response to the idea of 'being watched' – from those who welcome the opportunity for direct feedback to those who feel inhibited and very nervous at the prospect. The student's feelings – and yours – should be discussed openly and acknowledged.

Right from the start of the placement, it is helpful for the student to see *you* in practice. It gives the student a chance to get a 'feel' for the work, and it provides examples of practice for the two of you to discuss. It demonstrates your willingness to have your own practice appraised, and to practise what you preach; it shows you being positive and critical about your own work. Making direct observation a regular feature of those early days helps students to become comfortable with your presence, so they can take on more of a leading role in contacts with clients as their confidence increases. In this way, direct observation is not associated with assessment but with good learning practices.

In settings where direct observation is a regular feature of your work, there can be a problem in carving out a specific piece of work to focus on – there is so much 'material' that you are spoilt for choice. Planning is just as important in these circumstances, so that you do not let the opportunities drift by.

There is more about direct observation as a method of teaching in Chapter 18, pages 147–8.

Endings

Endings are notoriously difficult to handle, so we often try to ignore them, and fail to make best use of them. They receive much sketchier treatment in the practice teaching literature than beginnings: for example, Butler and Elliott (1985) discuss endings in work with clients, but not in relation to the placement; Bogo and Vayda (1987) and Ford and Jones (1987) each have a chapter on endings, but emphasize the psycho-social aspects of loss, separation and ritual.

It may seem strange to focus on endings at the same time as preparation for beginnings, only six chapters into this book. However, preparation for endings should begin at the beginning. This is achieved by being as clear as possible about what the programme, the practice teacher and the student expect the placement to offer. (Chapter 5 focuses on general expectations, and Chapters 13 and 14 on the specific content of the curriculum.)

Here are some of the different aspects to consider with regard to endings:

Ending the work with clients

Ideally, closure of work with a client should feel like a plane landing – relatively smooth, with a sense of 'arrival' and an understanding of where you are. In short, it should feel planned (Doel and Shardlow, 1993: 95–101). You aim to teach students to plan endings from the beginning of their contacts with clients. In addition to helping the student to learn good practice in closure, you have a responsibility to the agency's clients to make sure that they are offered a continuing service if this is wanted or required and available.

Reviewing the learning

The placement agreement should be kept under regular review, as a 'standing item' for the practice tutorial (see Chapter 16). Students should be asked to review the learning which they feel has come out of the placement (again, this will have been a continuing process during the placement). This also helps you to gain feedback about the placement from the student's point of view: did it offer adequate learning opportunities?

Summarizing the assessment

We will explore the question of assessment in detail later (Chapters 19, 20 and 21). At present, you need to be aware that assessment should not be a single event at the end of the placement marked by the final report; a concluding report should gather and summarize the assessments which have already occurred, so that the content of the report is not a surprise to you or the student at this stage.

Change in role

The end of the placement marks a change for both you and the student, and it pays to acknowledge this and to plan for it. The student, in particular, may start to disengage from the placement before it actually finishes; it helps to be aware of this process.

Rituals and unfinished business

Ford and Jones (1987: 44) consider four main tasks to be completed by placement end:

- bringing the work to a proper completion
- dealing with feelings
- working through any unfinished business
- a ritualized ending to the placement through ceremony

Each team has its own pattern of celebrating farewells, and these need to be sensitive to the particular student, but some kind of ritual to mark the ending is important.

Any unfinished business should be acknowledged, though you will have to use your judgement about the timing of this; very occasionally, it may be preferable to wait until after the placement is completed. The support of other practice teachers or college tutors is important, particularly if the placement has been a bruising one (e.g. where you have recommended that the student is not ready to practise; the sense of failure can feel very bitter). It is easier to draw on this support if you have developed these networks before or during the placement.

It is evident that the tasks associated with endings, as outlined above, are all bedded in beginnings and middles, too. If they seem to come out of the blue, it is likely that the ending will be unsatisfactory.

The practice teaching portfolio

In this section of your portfolio, you should demonstrate how you have prepared both for the beginning and ending of one or more placements. Rather than trying to describe every aspect of this preparation, focus on a few elements which have been a learning experience for you and how they have influenced your future practice teaching.

Examples of any orientation programmes which you have developed can be included in the portfolio (perhaps as an appendix?), including your evaluation of *how* it was used.

Example 6

Rita is a white practice teacher preparing a placement for Carla, a black student. Rita's agency is predominantly white, and there is no established group for black workers. Rita and Carla both had concerns about the lack of an available network for Carla, but nevertheless they decided to go ahead with the placement, which offered many interesting learning opportunities for Carla.

Rita described in her portfolio how the orientation programme she had already prepared for a previous (white) student was revised for Carla, in order to build in contact with other black workers (in this case, mainly in other agencies). Carla's evaluation of the orientation programme, with some suggested changes, was included in the portfolio. She also described how much Carla had valued the 'welcome to the placement' card which Rita had placed on Carla's desk on the first day; she later described it as 'warming up their relationship very quickly'.

Rita decided to focus on a discussion which she and Carla had late in the placement about changing roles. This had proved especially significant for Carla, who was a student on an employment-based route, and had found the placement with Rita had given her a lot more confidence to return to her workplace with a strong sense of what was good practice. When she returned, she also felt confident to ask for recognition of her needs as a black worker, which she felt had not been addressed before. Carla noted that Rita had helped her to make the transition from the placement to the workplace and to make connections between her current learning and her future needs.

Module 3

Anti-oppressive Practice Teaching

7 Power and oppression

About Activity 7   Who am I?

Who am I? begins the process of locating your own social identity and developing the skills to name differences and check assumptions.

Purpose

Any introduction to power and oppression must begin with the relationship between the practice teacher and the student. Open communication about your own 'social identity' is the first step to looking at power and oppression at different levels – personal, cultural and structural.

Method

- Complete the *Who am I?* activity. You can do this on your own, but if you do it with others, check that you are all in agreement beforehand about how much you will share with each other.
- If you are doing the activity alone, make a written note of your reflections on the activity; with others, discuss your responses to the various categories.

Variations

You may want to return to *Who am I?* when you have considered the concept of multiple oppressions, introduced in Chapter 8 (page 61).

Who am I? is also a useful activity to complete with a student as an introduction to your own teaching on power and oppression.

Activity 7   Who am I?

Your personal biography is as unique as your fingerprint. Yet there are characteristics of your biography which make you feel similar to some people and different from others.

Get a blue pen and a red pen. In each pair of boxes, tick the one which describes you: use the *red* pen if you feel this characteristic gives you relatively *more* power and the *blue* pen if you think it gives you relatively *less* power. Add any other categories you want.

Female	☐	Black	☐	Old	☐
Male	☐	White	☐	Young	☐
Gay	☐	Practice teacher	☐	Middle class	☐
Heterosexual	☐	Student	☐	Working class	☐
Benefit receiver	☐	Married	☐	Manager	☐
Wage earner	☐	Unmarried	☐	Worker	☐
Meat eater	☐	Able-bodied	☐		
Vegetarian	☐	Physically challenged	☐		
Graduate	☐	Poor	☐		
Non-graduate	☐	Wealthy	☐		

(Adapted from an exercise presented at The Albany)

Which characteristics are relatively visible and which ones can you choose not to reveal – are they the relatively powerful ones or not?

Are there any characteristics which you feel ambivalent about, or difficult to decide?

If you are doing this with others, make sure you all agree beforehand what you are willing to share. It is interesting to know how many 'reds' and 'blues' different people have, even if you do not specify which these are.

Start the discussion by thinking how these categories can be variously described (e.g. woman; Caucasian; elderly; straight; carnivore; handicapped, etc.). Do different 'titles' confer different meanings? What do you think of your personal power profile, and what other characteristics of power would you like to add?

Notes for practice teachers

Social location

It is important for you and the student to be aware of your own and each other's social identity. Thompson (1993: 131) refers to this as 'social location', meaning the extent to which you experience oppression, describing four aspects of our identity which are affected by the various forms of oppression:

- alienation, isolation, marginalization
- economic position and life-chances
- confidence and self-esteem
- social expectations, career opportunities, etc.

How much do you think you should disclose to your students, and how much do you expect them to disclose? Some identities are more 'visible' than others and are already in the public domain; others, like sexuality, may not be. Power, oppression and social location are not easy to discuss, and openness is important if the communication between you is to become genuine and not 'gamesy'.

Levels of inequality and discrimination

Thompson (1993: 19–22) looks at three different levels when analysing power and oppression: the 'P' level, which stands for personal; the 'C' for cultural level; and the 'S' for structural level. Social work has traditionally concerned itself with the personal level, but Thompson argues that we have a responsibility to be aware of inequality, discrimination and oppression at all three levels.

Here are some examples of what the three levels might mean for you as a practice teacher.

Personal level

An awareness of the potential for prejudice – for example, not understanding the needs of a student who is a lone parent, in terms of her or his child care responsibilities; or responding in stereotypical ways in terms of the gender of the lone parent – mother or father.

Cultural level

An awareness of shared ways of seeing, thinking and doing, and the differences between these – for example, assuming that a student will be celebrating Christmas, or failing to understand a Muslim student's need to return home before sunset during Ramadan.

Structural level

An awareness of the impact of broader social forces and policies on oppression – for example, matchmaking in placements, where practice teacher and student 'choose' each other, is usually seen as an ideal to work towards (even though, in fact, it is made difficult by shortages); however, this kind of matchmaking could be seen as reinforcing institutional oppression if – as the evidence suggests – individuals are likely to choose 'one of us'. Out-groups would find it even harder to get in. (The literature on interviewing for jobs certainly suggests this; see Collinson, 1988: 7–8.)

Naming differences

What makes it difficult to name differences? The tendency for people to search for commonalities is very strong; at social gatherings, individuals will often seek out others who look like themselves, and in conversation, people have a desire to make links with what is being said ('Funny you should say that because I had a similar experience myself . . .'). It is almost as though the conversation is being 'knitted' and there is a fear that it might become unravelled by any expressions of difference.

However, the desire to feel connected has adverse consequences if it leads to a 'colour-blind' approach, where differences are ignored. In these circumstances, people who are seen as members of an out-group are assimilated, but the cost of such assimilation is dear and includes the loss of social identities. A patient will express his racism by ignoring the colour of his admired doctor, claiming that she is not typical of her racial group – an exception who proves the rule.

It is essential that differences are named and valued, and that the power differentials are recognized. There may be many similar experiences which a black person and a white person share – the birth of a child, the loss of a partner – these are their commonalities, but their blackness or whiteness will have had a very different impact on each life. It is significant that white persons will probably be less aware of their whiteness than black persons are of their blackness, and this reinforces the power of the in-group at the further expense of the out-group.

Turning the tables on oppression

Placing emphasis on oppression is not without its dangers. Perhaps the most significant of these is the risk of heightening weaknesses at the expense of strengths. This in itself can be oppressive and feel patronizing. Many people have found ways of turning the tables on oppression – for example, the conventional credit card issued by the Dallas Gay Alliance uses the pink triangle, which was the symbol the Nazis made homosexuals wear in the concentration camps. Using such a symbol is a positive assertion by the Dallas gay community, as is the reclamation of the word 'queer' by some gay groups.

Disability groups in the UK have been assertive about moving the debate away from a sense of needy individuals with impairments, to the problem of a society which is disabling and which refuses to meet the different needs of its members. For example, there is increasing support for their assertion that it is the built environment which is disabling, and the Disabled People's Movement is a strong definer of the language used to describe disabled people, challenging the medical model of terminology based on illness and handicap (see Chapter 9).

From adjustment to empowerment

Should students who bring difference to the worksite make adjustments to fit in? Of course, some kind of accommodation between practice teacher, student and team will be necessary, but in these negotiations it is important to be aware of where power lies – or perhaps, more accurately, where *powers* lie. And it is not always with the practice teacher. A gay practice teacher found herself under attack from a straight student, who in turn found the homosexuality of her practice teacher threatening.

How able is your worksite to welcome a student who uses a wheelchair? Should a student who is disabled be expected to fit in? Thompson (1993: 109) describes how each one of us needs a *structure of aiding*: 'how many people could lead a "normal" life without everyday aids such as pens, cars, telephones, watches, cutlery, reading glasses, stairs and so on?'

The structure of aiding will be different for a person with an impairment – different, not special. If a disabled student's needs for aid can be seen in this light, we can see how the student is not a person who needs 'aid', but the worksite is a place which should provide opportunity for people with different needs for aid. This locates the problem not with the student but with the built environment and the agency which built it. This is a process which empowers rather than oppresses or victimizes.

Implications for practice teaching

Anti-oppressive practices in social work education should begin at the point of access to training. Writing about the absence of any real failure rates on training programmes, Baird comments that 'the profession is not able to take many risks in admission policy, and so courses mainly admit "normal", upwardly mobile, white, lower middle class graduates in their middle twenties. If there was a real quality assurance on practice competence it would be possible to admit more older, uneducated or disadvantaged applicants' (Baird, 1991: 26). The risks of filling the profession with individuals from the in-group are even greater.

Discussing selection interviews for students wishing to join social work courses, Brummer (1988) describes how black and white ways of handling anxiety can differ, given the inequalities in the power structure, and how these can be misinterpreted. Conceptions of the social work role are culture-specific, and if these differences are not acknowledged and valued, the prospects for practice learning and practice teaching are doomed. Part of this process includes the use of language, whose significance is discussed in Chapter 9 (pages 66–7).

Anti-oppressive practice teaching means recognizing, naming and valuing differences, while not sentimentalizing them. It means challenging stereotypes, checking assumptions and keeping anti-oppressive practice and practice teaching on the agenda, even when it gets uncomfortable.

The practice teaching portfolio

Describe how you have named differences with a student you have taught. If you have experience with a number of students, how has this process differed from student to student? Give specific examples to show how you taught about different levels of oppression (for example, the *personal*, *cultural* and *structural* levels described on pages 51–2) and how students have put their learning into practice.

   Can you develop an activity to help the student focus on one particular dimension of oppression, or use an existing exercise? Include this in your portfolio with a commentary about how you used it with the student.

Example 7

Raqia is a student in her early twenties on placement with Sandy in a home for older people. Sandy has developed an activity to introduce the concept of ageism.

   Sandy gave Raqia a number of common assumptions or equations about elders in Western societies, taken from Thompson (1993: 84–6):

- old = useless
- old = lonely
- old = childlike
- old = asexual
- old = not like children
- old = unintelligent
- old = ill
- old = poor
- old = not ill
- old = inhuman

Sandy did not ask Raqia to try to explain these equations (taken together, some appear to be contradictory), but to note down examples from her observations in the home over the next week which fit any of these categories. Through her observations, she made sense of most of these equations, and their oppressive effects become apparent to her in ways she had not been aware of before. Prior to the practice tutorial with Sandy, she read the chapter on ageism in Thompson (1993: 82–103), which cast some new light on the activity. During the session with Sandy, Raqia also reflected on the differences between Western views of age and those of her own culture, and the different value given to age in the two cultures.

   Sandy described and evaluated this work with Raqia in her portfolio.

---

8 Anti-racist practice teaching

About Activity 8   Cross currents

Cross currents looks at the possible dynamics associated with placements depending on the race of the practice teacher and the student. Obviously, race is just one factor in this dynamic, but it is a significant one.

Purpose

This chapter opens up the area of anti-racist practice teaching by asking you to isolate race as a dynamic in the practice teacher–student relationship. Although we are focusing on race in this particular chapter, it is expected that anti-oppressive practice teaching will be an explicit feature of other aspects of your work with the student (e.g. when considering how to create a climate for learning in Chapter 11).

Method

- Use the trigger words in the small box on page 56 to consider the issues for practice teachers and students in each of the four possibilities described at the top of the page and indicated in the large box.
- Think about the issues at a general level first, then consider particular examples. For this reason, the activity lends itself to group learning with other practice teachers, so you can bring in a variety of experiences and viewpoints.

Variations

Add your own trigger words to those on page 56 as you become aware of other areas which it is important to consider.

The same box can be used to look at the impact of other social divisions, such as gender (male practice teacher with female student, female practice teacher with female student, etc.).

Humphries et al. (1993: 64–9) provide a good source of background reading for *Cross currents*.

Activity 8   Cross currents

Are there particular issues which are likely to arise between a black practice teacher and a white student, between a black practice teacher and a black student, a white practice teacher and a white student, and a white practice teacher and a black student? What issues are likely to be common, and what issues are likely to be different?

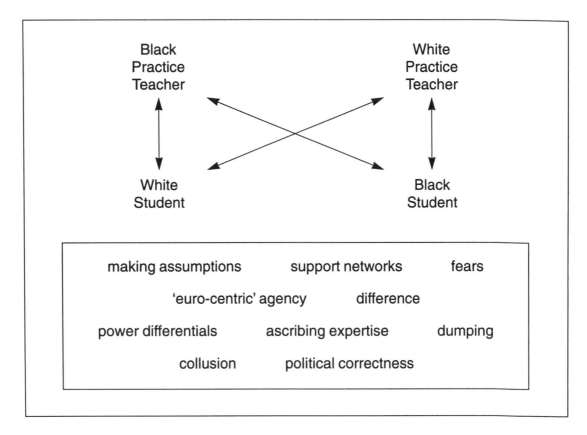

Use these triggers to help you consider the dynamics of same-race and different-race practice teacher–student relationships.

It might be helpful to consider each point at a general level first, then think about specific placements and specific experiences.

Notes for practice teachers

CCETSW Paper 30 (1991b) states that social workers at the point of qualification must be able to:

- demonstrate an awareness of both individual and institutional racism, and ways to combat both through anti-racist practice
- recognize and work with personal, racial, social and cultural differences
- understand and counteract the impact of discrimination
- work in an ethnically sensitive way

These are good intentions which require spelling out to put them into practice. Materials such as those provided by Coombe and Little (1986) and Humphries et al. (1993) are essential if, as a practice teacher, you are to know where to begin to teach anti-racist practice. We also need a framework – a model – to provide guidelines for action.

A model for developing anti-racist practice teaching

Shardlow and Doel (1993a) suggest a model for anti-racist practice teaching with these four elements:

- power
- the practice context
- the practice teacher's practice
- the practice curriculum

Power

How is power amplified or diminished in the relationship between practice teacher and student? (See 'Naming differences', Chapter 7, page 52). Assumptions can be wrongly made that issues of race are only relevant when a black student is offered a placement in a largely white agency, and not when white students and practice teachers meet.

The practice context

What is the context in which the placement occurs – in other words, how anti-racist are the agency's own practices? As a practice teacher, you have a responsibility to be aware of the practice context, even if you are not responsible for the context itself. Your assessment of the agency's 'biography' should be discussed with students to provide the backdrop for their learning. For example, Suzy is a white practice teacher working in a Family Centre where the staff are all female and white, though a significant number of the children and families who use the nursery are black. She is critical of many aspects of the Centre's practices, including its failure to recruit from the black community, and she often feels she is swimming upstream. *Anti-racist practices* in the Centre are in their infancy, but the opportunities for *anti-racist practice teaching* are enormous, and Suzy is able to make use of these by making the practice context a regular and open part of the teaching.

The practice teacher's practice

Practice teachers often enjoy the new theory and practices which are stimulated by exposure to students on placement. This is valid as long as it does not feel onerous to the student; certainly, no student should be expected to create anti-racist practice for themselves without guidance. It is important to be honest about the extent to which anti-racist practice is a feature of your own practice, and to acknowledge that there is no end-point at which practice can be considered perfect. Your own practice is developing alongside the student's, but you are not relying on the student to pull you along. In the case of Suzy in the Family Centre, it is only during the last two years or so that she has begun to use an anti-racist yardstick to question her own and colleagues' practices. Since then, she has asked her agency for training, she has made contact with local black groups, and she is reading the anti-racist literature more widely. These are signs that she sees her own learning as a mutual responsibility between herself and the agency.

The practice curriculum

The practice curriculum is the framework for the learning which will take place during the placement (see Chapters 13, 14, 15). You have a responsibility to provide opportunities for the student to learn about anti-racist practice in a practice setting, and to gather evidence to support your judgement about the student's abilities. However, the training programme as a whole has the task of making sure that anti-racist practice is a key feature of the course curriculum and finding ways of supporting your practice teaching – for example, by providing teaching materials and mechanisms for practice teachers to learn from each others' experiences, and a code of practice (see Ahmed et al., 1988, for a draft code).

Anti-racist practice should be an integrated aspect of the curriculum, not marginalized as a 'speciality'. Similarly, the practice curriculum and class curriculum need to be harmonized, so that the student has a coherent experience. This degree of integration is difficult, but it is more likely to be achieved when the curriculum is explicit; in these circumstances, student, practice teacher and tutor understand the expectations and can check how each aspect of the curriculum is combining to teach anti-racist practice.

Ethnic-sensitive practice

Devore and Schlesinger (1991) have developed a practice model founded on the concept of ethnic-sensitive practice. They describe the *ethnic reality*, which is a combination of class and ethnicity, and detail four basic assumptions of ethnic-sensitive practice:

- 'Individual and collective history have bearing on problem generation and solution.'
- 'The present is most important.'
- 'Nonconscious phenomena affect individual functioning.'

- 'Ethnicity is a source of cohesion, identity and strength as well as a source of strain, discordance and strife.' (Devore and Schlesinger, 1991: 180)

The Devore and Schlesinger model is one you might find useful to introduce into your practice teaching.

Affirmative practice

Bandana Ahmad discusses the notion of affirmative practice as a way of permeating non-racist practice in all aspects of planning:

> Affirmative practice is not about discriminating in favour of Black clients and disfavouring White clients and 'reversing discrimination'. On the contrary, it is about condoning and ensuring equity in social work planning for practice. It is about acknowledging the fact that as a result of past experiences of oppression and discrimination, Black clients have an accumulation of deficit. It is about redressing this deficit with affirmative practice, without which the gap of inequality will continue to widen, leaving Black clients even further behind. (Ahmad, 1990: 76–7)

Ahmad's description of affirmative practice in relation to anti-racist practice can be modified for anti-racist practice teaching:

- making personal time for working on components of good practice teaching, including identifying major deficiencies in personal practice
- having a specific personal goal for your anti-racist practice teaching
- analysing the differences between black and white students with same or similar strengths and weaknesses
- moving strongly away from a 'colour-blind' approach (e.g. if the problem is the same or similar then its impact on both black and white students is the same) to an 'ethnically sensitive' approach (e.g. analysing how the impact is both common and different)
- monitoring and articulating personal change, in terms of values and practice teaching

Ahmad (1990: 82–3) suggests a checklist to affirm black workers as a resource for change. This equally applies to the question of black workers as a support to black students on placements in agencies.

Unveiling

A powerful expression of oppression is the denial of the achievements of oppressed groups or individuals within the group. The re-discovery of historical persons as Black is part of the process which makes the achievements of black people visible and valued.

For example, the expression 'it's the real McCoy' is commonly understood, but how many people know that it originated with a black engineer, born in 1843 the son of Kentucky slaves, who fled to freedom in Canada? Elijah McCoy designed an automatic lubricating cup to prevent overheating of train engines, and by 1920 he had over fifty patents. Inspectors would ask 'Is it the real McCoy?' to ensure a machine had automatic lubrication; the engineer gave his name to an expression which stands as a sign of genuine quality, but few know, let alone assume, that he was black.

Unveiling the achievements of groups who are discriminated against is a powerful weapon against oppression. This is not limited to historical persons or movements; it is just as important that the achievements of black people and black groups are valued close to home, in social work agencies. This does not exclude valuing achievements of white workers, but – as Ahmad points out in connection with black clients – affirmative practice is necessary to redress a deficit.

Valuing the achievements of oppressed groups is not the same as valuing them *because* they are oppressed. White workers who continually seek advice from their black colleagues *because* they are black risk abusing them. When a black worker is valued for her specialist knowledge of the Criminal Justice Act or his ability to use sign language with deaf people, that is the time when black practitioners and white practitioners are seen in different roles and valued equally.

'There are no black students around here'

A white practice teacher in a sea of white faces might suggest that anti-racist practice teaching is not possible because 'there are no black students to teach'. This is a false notion in many respects.

First, is it a true perception? The practice teacher might perceive a sea of white faces, but has he or she looked carefully? It is important to challenge assumptions – for example, there were reports of horrific racist attacks on the black community in Norwich during 1992, yet conventional wisdom supposes that there are no black communities in a city like Norwich. Social work agencies staffed by white people can be unreceptive to black people, thus keeping black users at bay and reinforcing the idea that 'black communities look after themselves'. An agency cut off from local black communities is unlikely to attract black students.

Second, racism does not disappear when there are no black people. This attitude actually reinforces racism by suggesting that the 'problem' lies with black individuals. It is a view which fails to locate racism at the cultural and structural levels (see Chapter 7), and – at the personal level – it dangerously identifies racism as a problem imported by the individual black student.

Anti-racist practice teaching is both possible and essential in all circumstances; the opportunities do not disappear when a white practitioner is teaching a white student working with a white client, nor does the need for anti-racist practice teaching diminish. The potential loss when same-race people are working together is the opportunity to develop ethnic-sensitive practice teaching. In these circumstances, it is necessary to look for possible links with other oppressions (e.g. a practice teacher helped a student to make this kind of connection when the student worked with a London family who faced hostile 'regionalism' on an estate in a northern city).

Avoiding hierarchies of oppression

Who am I? (Chapter 7, page 50) revealed the complexity of social identity. Most people have a mix of red and blue ticks, feeling relatively powerful and relatively powerless in different situations. It is important that these complexities do not become a competitive game of 'Who is the most oppressed?': the straight black man versus the gay white woman; the old white woman versus the young black youth. Thompson (1993) discusses the concept of multiple oppressions, rejecting a hierarchy of social divisions in which we are forced to decide which oppressed group has priority.

Instead, we must think about commonalities and differences. Black people in the UK have a common experience of oppression in a way that white people do not; however, there are parallel experiences of oppression in other social groups (e.g. older people) and there are different experiences of oppression within one group (e.g. the black Conservative candidate for Cheltenham in the 1992 General Election and a black unemployed youth in Brixton). There are different perspectives and common perceptions. Understanding these differences and commonalities is essential for anti-racist practice teaching.

The practice teaching portfolio

Take one of the frameworks described in this chapter to evaluate your own anti-racist practice teaching. Make sure you relate it to your actual practice (what you did and why), rather than to good intentions, and feel open to reflect on the difficulties and the things which did not work too well; the portfolio is not intended to be an account of perfect practice.

Anti-oppressive practice teaching is not confined to one part of your portfolio. Remember to weave anti-oppressive themes into all aspects of the portfolio.

Example 8

Shirley and Yusef are black practice teachers, working in a largely white social work agency. Shirley is Afro-Caribbean and Yusef is Pakistani, and they are both members of a small support group which brings the few black workers in the agency together. It is a good forum to promote anti-racist practice teaching.

Shirley and Yusef are each completing a practice teaching portfolio, and they have combined some of their practice teaching sessions with two white students, Vicki and Margaret, who are on placement with them. They used an exercise developed by two black trainers, Dave Henry and Yvonne Channer, to trigger discussion about black and white perspectives about how professional boundaries are drawn. These are the trigger questions:

continued

What would you do if:

1   Through community networks, you become aware that one of your clients is selling cannabis, and possibly heroin.
2   You are asked to visit a family in which there is vague concern relating to child care issues. In reading the file information, you realize that this family has very tenuous links with sections of your own extended family.
3   A friend who is the lone parent of two young children asks you to write a letter for her in support of her application for a nursery place for her youngest child. She does not want 'formal' social work contact.

(Dave Henry and Yvonne Channer)

In asking the students to develop dos and don'ts as principles to help promote good practice, Shirley and Yusef also helped to unfold the stereotypes held by the white students. They demonstrated anti-racist practice teaching by discussing both their commonalities and their differences as black practitioners. Vicki and Margaret were able to see their commonalities as white students, but also their differences. They were able to use this analysis in their work with clients, and to transpose it to other social divisions, such as the commonalities and differences between Shirley, Vicki and Margaret as women and Yusef as a man.

Shirley and Yusef each gave their own description of this process in their portfolios, as an example of anti-racist practice teaching.

9 Cultural competence

About Activity 9 Just a joke?

Just a joke? skates the thin line between humour and offence. This mirrors the knife edge between oppression and empowerment which characterizes social work practice, and the fine line between cultural competence and political correctness. *Just a joke?* introduces you to these important issues for practice teaching. *(Just a joke? (1)* is on page 64; *Just a joke? (2)* is on page 69.)

Purpose

This module develops an understanding of the idea of a continuum of cultural competence. The continuum is relevant to individuals, agencies and to broader social institutions. As a practice teacher it is important to develop your own cultural competence.

Method

- Read *Just a joke? (1)* on page 64. What is your initial response? Write a few brief comments to yourself before turning to page 69.
- Turn to page 69; try to forget your response to the first cartoon and read *Just a joke? (2)*. What is your initial response to this cartoon?
- Bring your thoughts about the two cartoons together. What are the differences – if any – between your responses to these two cartoon strips?

Variations

If *Just a joke?* is used in a group, participants can divide into two or more groups (perhaps separated into gender groups), discussing one or other of the cartoons. If there are enough participants, you can have single-sex groups of men and women looking at one each of the cartoons (in other words, a total of four groups). Ask each group for its response.

Participants will no doubt discuss sexism, but how many pick up on issues of heterosexism, since each cartoon assumes none of its characters is gay?

Activity 9   Just a joke (1)

With acknowledgements to 'Banshee' by Mandie Fletcher and Debbie Clark (The *Guardian*)

Make a note of your response to this cartoon before turning to page 69.

Notes for practice teachers

A six-stage continuum of cultural competence

Cultural competence is a notion which helps us to think about the 'behaviours, attitudes and policies that come together in a system, agency or among professionals, and enable [them] to work effectively in cross-cultural situations' (Cross et al., 1989: 13). Cross and his colleagues at the Native American Child Welfare Association in Portland, Oregon use the word 'competence' 'because it implies having the capacity to function effectively'.

There are six stages on the continuum:

Cultural destructiveness is the purposeful destruction of a culture – for example, the exclusion of the Welsh language from schools in the nineteenth century, or present day immigration laws which separate families.

Cultural incapacity is characterized by patronizing beliefs about the cultural superiority of the dominant culture of helpers. Personnel practices in these agencies are discriminatory, and the morale of people from other cultures is low.

Cultural blindness is at the midpoint of the curriculum. A liberal philosophy of equal approach to everybody has the intention of being unbiased, but implicitly believes in the 'rightness' of the dominant culture's approach. Cultural blindness encourages assimilation and denies differences – for example, failing to take account of different religious practices of workers in an agency.

Cultural pre-competence is a realization that the agency's services are in need of improvement for a specific population, and shows the first steps to addressing this need. However, there are dangers of tokenism if progress is not sustained to the next stage.

Cultural competence is the recognition and acceptance of diversity. It is coupled with an active self-assessment at individual, agency and societal level. A culturally competent agency is marked by variety and adaptations to service models, employing staff from different cultures who are committed to their own culture but able to work with others.

Cultural proficiency holds culture in high esteem, adding to the knowledge base of culturally competent practice by conducting research, developing new approaches based on culture and disseminating the results of demonstration projects. Culturally proficient staff and agencies are advocates for cultural competence throughout the system.

The continuum can be used to assess the current competence of an agency or individual, as a prelude to progress to the next stage. It is a journey with staging posts and without end, because expectations of what is cultural proficiency are always changing.

Language and political correctness

Language is a central element in the notion of cultural competence, and it is a battleground where oppression is constructed and reinforced. There have been some notable successes in attempts to reform language in ways which are less oppressive, with important victories for language groups such as Welsh-speakers.

The power of exclusion is one of the most significant aspects of language, most notably in a sentence like 'When the reader has finished the book he should return it to the library', which makes honorary men out of half the population. The *Encyclopaedia Britannica* has a famous entry – 'for Wales, see England' – which has a similar subsuming effect.

Male gender-specific language is very common, but there are more subtle ways in which language oppresses certain groups. Thompson (1993: 86) quotes from a local Alcohol Forum in which a psychiatrist discusses safe limits for weekly alcohol consumption: 'safety limits are proposed in terms of alcohol units per week (10) but these limits are for males and females, not for the elderly'. The distinction between 'ordinary people' and 'the elderly' is subtly but clearly made.

Even when awareness is heightened, it is not always obvious what is correct. For example, the term 'nitty-gritty' may be a reference to the nits and grit in the hair of black slave women after they had been raped in the cotton fields by white slave-owners. Does this mean that we should bury the phrase, as a mark of respect for the appalling events it commemorates; or is the reverse true – do we use the phrase to show that we do not forget the horrors of slavery? Or is it just another phrase whose original significance is becoming increasingly obscure?

Language reformers have met hostility in their attempts to influence the way we speak as a means of changing the way we think. This opposition has been powerfully expressed through ridicule, and though this can partly be explained as a predictable reaction by oppressors, it is also an understandable response to the tendency of language reform to sound clumsy, euphemistic or even autocratic (as in the 'thought police'). Below are terms adapted from an article in the *Guardian* (5 January 93). What makes you agree with some, laugh at others, or just feel puzzled?

- *chronologically gifted* – old
- *aurally inconvenienced* – deaf
- *total visual impairment* – blind
- *speech impaired* – dumb
- *differently abled* – physically disabled
- *differently sized* – little or large
- *exceptional* – mentally impaired
- *intellectually challenged* – mentally handicapped

continued

- *alternative dentation* – false teeth
- *horizontally challenged* – fat
- *hair disadvantaged* – bald
- *sex worker* – prostitute
- *melanin impoverished* – white
- *a person of colour* – coloured
- *Black* – black

Authorship

The power of language is not just the words we use, but who decides *which* words we use – the prime definers. Black youths on a bus may shout 'niggers' as a term of abuse to rival black youths on a street corner, but they are the authors of their own words. The power equation is brutally different when white youths or white police use that same term. The Dallas Gay Alliance chooses to embrace a symbol associated with the brutal treatment of homosexuals by the Nazis, and some homosexual groups are reclaiming the term 'queer' as a positive assertion (see Chapter 7).

In 1992, BBC radio's *In Touch* surveyed people with sight difficulties to discover what term they would prefer to describe their impairment. There was no consensus. 'Blind', 'unsighted', 'sightless', 'partially-sighted', 'vision-impaired', 'visually handi-capped', 'hard-of-seeing' – all attracted support and hostility in roughly equal measure. It is clear that the message coming from that survey is the importance at the individual level of letting people be the authors of their own language, even if this is different from the language we choose to use at a cultural or structural level of discourse.

Implications for anti-oppressive practice teaching

What are the implications of the notion of cultural competence for practice teaching? First, at a personal level, it is important for you and the student to be aware of your own social location, to challenge stereotypes and to value difference (see Chapter 7). Authorship of your own social descriptions (student and practice teacher) is impor-tant, too. Contrasts and similarities in your social locations should be discussed openly and reviewed during the placement.

Second, the issue of power in your own relationships should be on the table (practice teacher–student, student–colleagues, practice teacher–colleagues, etc.). It is important to challenge assumptions (e.g. that the practice teacher is always relatively more powerful than the student).

Third, as a practice teacher, you need to think at a structural level as well as at the personal and cultural levels (see page 51). Use the continuum on page 65 to start an inventory of your agency's cultural competence, focusing on how the organization's policies increase or decrease opportunities for oppressed groups. Regular analysis of the way broader social divisions construct and maintain oppression is important for the student's learning, but it is also necessary to avoid rhetoric and to look close to home for the chance to challenge oppressive practices.

That begins with you.

The practice teaching portfolio

In your portfolio, include an example of your teaching about an aspect of cultural competence, and what kind of impact this had on the student's practice. The example below looks specifically at the idea of *authorship* which is discussed on page 67.

Example 9

Suzanne, the student, described how she used the concept of *authorship*, introduced in a practice tutorial, to explore with a person who has multiple sclerosis what language he preferred to use to describe himself, and how the use of different kinds of terms affected him.

Suzanne wrote a few paragraphs for Rick, her practice teacher, to include in his portfolio about the way she understood the idea of *authorship*, as taught by him.

Rick described the benefits Suzanne saw from the idea of *authorship*, and the difficulties she had in using it. However, Suzanne's own words were the most powerful testimony to the effectiveness of Rick's teaching.

Activity 9   Just a joke? (2)

(With acknowledgements to Phil Page, a *Guardian* reader)

Make a brief note of your response to this cartoon. How does it compare to your response to the first cartoon on page 64?

Module 4

Models of Learning

10 Giving and receiving feedback

About Activity 10   Between pussyfoot and overkill

Between pussyfoot and overkill presents fifteen opportunities for giving feedback, and in each case you are asked to consider what you would say, if anything.

Purpose

Feedback is an essential element in practice teaching. Knowing how to give feedback to students in ways which they will 'hear' is vital in order to develop their practice skills. Similarly, it is important for you to seek feedback from the student about your practice teaching skills, to help you develop them.

Method

Read each of the situations on page 74 in turn.

- If possible, relate each example to a particular instance, and think about your initial response.
- Decide whether you would say anything to the person or people in question. If not, why not? Be honest with yourself.
- In those situations where you would give feedback, how would you do this and when? Rehearse the words you would use.
- Return to this activity after you have read the notes on pages 74–8.

Variations

Between pussyfoot and overkill lends itself to small groupwork, where people can compare their decisions and work out responses together.

Over the course of a week, gather similar examples from your own work setting; then you can use these examples with students as a way of developing their skills in feedback.

Activity 10   Between pussyfoot and overkill

Consider each of the situations below. Would you make any comment? If not, why not? If so, how would you phrase your comment?

- A close colleague has bad breath.
- Your team leader has changed her hairstyle, and you think it's a great improvement.
- A colleague has a habit of interrupting you at unit meetings.
- The secretary typed a report particularly quickly.
- You hear a team colleague being curt and unhelpful over the phone.
- Your student arrives punctually on the first day of the placement.
- The secretary types your letter to Ms Bartlett as Miss Bartlett.
- You see a colleague handling a tricky situation with a resident very well.
- In a meeting with senior managers, your boss fails to acknowledge your contribution to a policy document which bears his name.
- One of your colleagues has had an article published in *Community Care*.
- You dislike your team leader's tendency to hover around you when he wants your attention when you are on the phone.
- Your student comes to the first day of the placement wearing a 'Proud to Be Gay' badge.
- You suspect a student placed with a colleague is using the phone for a lot of personal calls.
- In team meetings, you feel many of your contributions are not listened to or built on.
- Your team leader has changed his hairstyle, and you think it's a great improvement.

Return to these examples after you have read the notes on pages 74–8 and see if there are any changes to your responses.

Notes for practice teachers

Affirming feedback and challenging feedback

The art of giving and receiving feedback is not well developed in the UK. Positive feedback is too often viewed suspiciously as 'not genuine' and taken for flattery or deference. Negative feedback is frequently avoided in case it is hurtful or leads to a defensive counter-attack. On those occasions when feedback is given, it is more likely to be when things are going wrong rather than right, so it is negative and it has no history of positive feedback to underpin it. All in all, it seems a lot safer not to bother with too much feedback, yet in the long run this is the more dangerous policy.

'Positive' and 'negative' are not useful terms to describe different kinds of feedback. Feedback well given should always have a positive intention and outcome, even when it is 'negative'. It is better to think of feedback which *affirms* and feedback which *challenges*, each with a desire for a positive result.

Of course, you are giving and receiving messages all the time. Whether these are verbal or non-verbal, intended or unconscious, understood or misunderstood, explicit or obscure, the messages are there. Unfortunately, prevailing forms of communication are often understated, open to mistranslation and frequently coded; indeed, there seems to be a special admiration for people who can say something whilst actually meaning the opposite (like Michael Heseltine's coded opposition during the Thatcher years). The limitations, even dangers, of this form of communication have yet to be widely accepted.

Giving feedback and receiving feedback are essential skills for a practice teacher, and the good news is that they can be learned and improved upon. This activity develops skills in explicit, deliberate, verbal feedback.

Stages in giving feedback

1 Becoming aware of your own style of giving feedback

What are your own experiences of giving feedback? The first stage is to sample your own style and frequency of giving feedback. Do you give feedback regularly? Make a note of the occasions over the last two days or so when you gave deliberate, direct feedback – to a student, a colleague, a friend, a member of your family – and ask yourself whether you found it relatively easy or difficult. Are there any patterns? For example, do you tend to give more feedback to women than to men, or vice versa? Were there occasions when you wanted to give feedback but did not, and what prevented you? Are the examples of you giving affirming feedback and challenging feedback roughly balanced, or do you give more of one than the other?

2 Preparing groundrules beforehand

As a practice teacher, there is an expectation that you will be giving feedback about the student's practice during the placement. It is better to make some contractual agreement about this from the beginning, so that you and the student have a common understanding of how and why there will be feedback. If communication can be viewed as a kind of game (in the best sense of the word), the need for rules becomes obvious; giving feedback without establishing these groundrules is like letting football players loose on to a pitch without rules. In those circumstances, people do get hurt. The rules of a game like football are non-negotiable, whereas the groundrules for giving feedback should be negotiated between you and the student.

3 Understanding the impact of differences in power

The channels of communication which are necessary for feedback may be blocked by differences, or perceived differences, in power. This is why it is important for the system and pattern of giving and receiving feedback to be negotiated openly, with acknowledgement of power differences. Similarly, any personal and cultural differences in patterns of giving and receiving feedback should be discussed.

4   *Being clear about the purpose of the feedback*

What is the aim of giving the feedback? If feedback is given manipulatively rather than assertively, it is unlikely to be helpful or effective. Manipulative feedback has an ulterior motive: perhaps to 'soften up', as a prelude to some kind of request, or to discharge your own feelings and frustrations. Assertive feedback is given to students to help them to understand the impact of their behaviour, not to make you feel better.

Being clear about the purpose helps you decide whether or not to give the feedback, and it helps you consider how welcome the feedback will be. How receptive is the receiver likely to be, especially if the feedback is of the challenging kind? What are the consequences of *not* giving feedback?

5   *Seeking the views of the person to whom you are going to give feedback*

It can be irritating for students if they hear you say what they already know – in other words, they know they should not have said something and they do not need to have you point it out. On the other hand, you need to be careful not to set them a trap, by asking students for their own self-assessment only to follow it with your own damning appraisal. Avoid the 'just enough rope to hang yourself' school of social work learning.

It is preferable to say something like: 'As we agreed, I'm going to give you some feedback about your court report, some of it affirming and some of it challenging, but I thought it was only fair to ask you what you thought about it first. Is that how you would like to begin?' (see Shardlow, 1988). The student might still prefer to hear your comments first, but is likely to value the chance to decide.

6   *Being specific and giving reasons*

The feedback we give can be too general to be helpful, such as: 'I thought that was very good' or 'I didn't like your general attitude.' Translate these into 'It was good when you said ... because ...' or 'I didn't find it helpful when you ... because ...' and a dialogue can begin, especially if you follow the statement with '... and I wondered what you thought about that?'

7   *The keep/change rule*

Rather than inviting feedback in the form of what was good and what was bad, or what did you like and what did you dislike, it is better to frame the feedback so that it is likely to have positive results and to be seen as helpful, even when it is challenging. It is useful to give feedback in terms of 'what I would keep' and 'what I would change'.

When somebody gives feedback (e.g. in a training or supervision session), it is common to see this following pattern: a general positive, followed by specific negatives – for example, 'Well, in general it was fine, but I think you could have said more about the background theory.' This pattern should be countered by agreeing a rule with your students that you will both make sure that a specific 'what I would keep' statement always comes before a specific 'what I would change' statement.

It is also common for people to find it difficult to make affirming comments about themselves. Sticking to the 'keep/change' rule encourages students to be assertive.

8   *Review the feedback groundrules*

It is important to keep the feedback process under review. Does the student feel appropriately challenged by the way you are giving feedback (in other words, stretched and supported at the same time)? By doing this, you are showing the skills of *receiving* feedback, which is the focus of the next section.

Stages in receiving feedback

1   *Being aware of your own response to receiving feedback*

Sampling your own responses to receiving feedback is the first step to understanding the likely responses of other people, including your student. Do you seek feedback actively, or do you tend to shy away from it? Make a note of occasions during the last few days when you have received affirming feedback and challenging feedback; how did your responses to each of these differ?

2   *Asking for feedback*

The student is likely to see your behaviour as a model, so it is important to show an interest in feedback. It can be particularly difficult for students to give feedback to practice teachers because of the difference in power, status and experience (see Chapter 7). However, there are parallels in your two situations: just as the student is learning about practice, you are learning about practice teaching. This knowledge goes some way towards equalizing the relationship.

Your willingness to receive feedback gives the student practice in giving it, and the content of the feedback is usually very valuable to your development as a practice teacher.

3   *Not becoming defensive*

Defensiveness is a frequent response to feedback. Challenging feedback is often delivered as criticism, and received as negative, which triggers a defence of the perceived 'shortcoming'. As a receiver of the student's feedback, listen carefully and without comment until the student has made her or his point; if students follow the groundrules, they will have made a specific 'keep' as well as a specific 'change', which in itself reduces the tendency to become defensive. If they failed to keep to the groundrules, you can remind them of this and ask them to start again.

Treating the feedback as a valuable source of information rather than as a personal criticism is a way of discovering more about yourself. Asking students about practical suggestions for changes, rather than giving an explanation of why you did what you did, is more likely to help you both.

4   Responding to unfair feedback

There are times when we are at the receiving end of challenging feedback which is given in the heat of the moment, and not played according to the rules. The student's feedback might feel like a blatant misreading of the situation. You may suspect that it is manipulative, that the student does not actually mean what he or she is saying, but is using the opportunity as a platform for other issues. How do you deal with this kind of unfair feedback?

It is important to establish a clear understanding of what the student is saying and what alternatives are being proposed. If you are feeling a bit vulnerable on the day, or have had more than your fair share of criticism recently, you will be particularly sensitive and might off-load these other frustrations onto an unsuspecting student. It is important not to deny the student's perceptions, but to let him or her know that yours are different, and to find out what the gap is and why it exists. If you suspect that the student is using the feedback to express feelings from elsewhere (e.g. their anger at an earlier piece of work with which you were not satisfied), it is important to check this out. The quickest way to stop game-playing (as opposed to 'playing the game') is to point to it openly and directly.

5   Sweeping up later

Receiving bruising feedback is unpleasant, and it colours your next contacts with the student. Acknowledging the bruise at some later date and reflecting back on what was said is an important step towards re-opening communication channels. Was it the content of the feedback which was unfair, or the rule-breaking, or both? Start this process by each of you summarizing the other person's position as fairly as possible. This is also a good time to review the process of giving and receiving feedback, to renegotiate the groundrules.

6   Reporting on changes brought about by feedback

Giving and receiving feedback requires skill, energy, risk and trust – is it worth it? The link in the feedback loop is completed when you find out how a piece of feedback has altered your student's work, or when you let your students know how their feedback has influenced your practice teaching. In those circumstances, both of you learn the true value of feedback.

The practice teaching portfolio

In this chapter, you have been learning about two kinds of feedback – *affirming feedback* and *challenging feedback* (often misleadingly called 'positive feedback' and 'negative feedback'). There is another dimension to consider – *assertive feedback* and *manipulative feedback*.

Assertive feedback is given with the receiver's purposes in mind, while manipulative feedback is given for other reasons, which are usually destructive (dumping your own feelings, seeking retribution, exercising power over somebody, etc.).

Describe instances of these four kinds of feedback from your experiences with a student on placement with you. How did your understanding of different kinds of feedback help you to teach the student how to develop skills in this area?

Example 10

Vincent was a student on placement with Dave in a drop-in centre for people with mental health problems. Vincent and Dave agreed groundrules for giving feedback at the beginning of the placement, including the keep/change rule (page 76). They rehearsed this in practice teaching sessions, and Vincent was invited to use the same formula to give Dave feedback about how he was finding Dave's teaching style and methods. He was able to use the keep/change formula, and seemed happy with it.

Some weeks into the placement, Dave received feedback from one of his colleagues that Vincent had told the colleague that he didn't think Dave was giving him enough theory in the sessions. Dave was angry and hurt to hear this from a colleague, especially since he had specifically given Vincent the time and opportunity to express this in the sessions. He also felt a bit embarrassed that this kind of message was being relayed by a colleague. However, he thanked the colleague and let him know that he was curious about why Vincent had not told him directly.

In his portfolio, Dave described how he raised this issue with Vincent, the learning they both took from the experience, and how it influenced his practice teaching. He discussed Elgin's concept of 'syntonics' – which is basically getting in tune with people, using a shared communication channel – and how this seemed to take a long time between himself and Vincent (Elgin, 1989: 25). Dave also included a brief account, written by Vincent, of how Dave taught him to develop assertive feedback.

11 Learning styles

About Activity 11   Knit one . . .

Knit one . . . is a fun way to discover how adults learn – what helps and what hinders our learning. A practical demonstration of teaching a manual skill (knitting) opens up the broad issue of different teaching and learning styles and how to create a good climate for learning.

Purpose

We all have different ways of learning. A practice teacher needs to be able to adapt to each individual student's style and to help to extend the student's repertoire. This activity provides a trigger for a group of practice teachers to consider what helps and what hinders learning.

Method

- This is a group activity, best done with six to twelve participants. Explain the purpose to the group, in terms of a trigger to think about what helps and what hinders learning.
- Gather the props together and ask for two volunteers: a knitter and a non-knitter. The knitter will be teaching the non-knitter how to knit.
- Observers need pen and paper to make notes as the teaching session progresses.
- Give the teacher a minute or so to collect thoughts, and five to ten minutes for the actual demonstration.
- Give people a minute to finish their notes before asking for feedback, first from the knitter and the learner, then from the observers. Take notes on a flip-chart (under the headings 'help' and 'hinder'); look for differences as well as commonalities, so the group draws out themes about the different and similar ways in which people learn.
- Stick with the knitting analogy to begin with, moving on to the parallels with social work practice teaching and learning later. (The notes on pages 84–8 provide prompts.)

Variations

Knit one ... is designed for a group of people. You can use this activity with other practice teachers, with colleagues in your team and with students. If you find it difficult to organize a small group, use the learning styles questionnaire described in the portfolio section (page 89).

Activity 11   Knit one . . .

This activity is best carried out in a small group. However, it is possible to use video to record yourself teaching another person a practical skill.

The small group will be observing a short demonstration of a 'teacher' and a 'learner'. The teacher will be teaching the learner how to knit.

Props

- a pair of medium to large size knitting needles
- a ball of brightly-coloured, easy-to-handle wool
- a flip-chart and marker pen
- two volunteers – one who can knit and one who cannot

Arrangements

- four to ten observers in a 'horseshoe', with two chairs for the volunteers in the gap of the 'horseshoe'; each observer needs pen and paper
- at least thirty minutes to complete the activity and to discuss it

Process

- Allow the knitter-teacher a minute or two to decide how she (or, rarely, he) will go about the task.
- Explain to the rest of the group that they will be watching five to ten minutes of the experienced knitter teaching the novice knitter. On the left-hand side of a sheet of paper, each observer will make a note of what they thought *helped* the learner, and on the right-hand side a note of what they thought *hindered* the learner.
- After the demonstration, these observations will be shared, and you will write them on the flip-chart, drawing out themes which have relevance for social work practice teaching and learning.

See the notes on pages 84–8 for a commentary on the learning which comes from this activity.

Notes for practice teachers

How do adults learn best? This is a complex question, and the answer will vary from one individual to another. Honey and Mumford (1986) describe four styles of learning – activist, pragmatist, theorist and reflector – and you may want to complete their questionnaire in order to discover your own learning styles profile. Gardiner (1989: 66–70 and 128–30) identifies deep/holistic and surface/serialistic approaches to learning. The *Knit one . . .* exercise is a way of teasing out some of the answers to the question of how adults learn; it is an example of learning by a mix of doing and reflecting.

Getting the best out of *Knit one ...*

Use of metaphor and analogy

A metaphor can help to throw fresh light on a subject. *Knit one ...* takes a manual skill and asks you to suspend thoughts about teaching and learning social work. Other relatively simple practical skills, such as typewriting skills, can substitute for knitting if need be. However, it is necessary to make the links between the learning in *Knit one ...* and the learning in social work in order to complete the activity. In many respects, *the act of learning equals the act of making connections*, and the use of a metaphor such as *Knit one ...* mobilizes our ability to make creative links of thought.

Eleven core themes are summarized below, accompanied by the parallels with teaching social work practice. These are borne out of many sessions with the wool and needles! When you have completed *Knit one ...*, turn to the notes below to see if these are the themes which you highlighted. No doubt you will be able to add to the list.

Previous experience

Few knitters asked the learner about previous practice which might be relevant – for example, any activities which involved similar fine motor skills. In one example, the learner confessed that he had always considered himself to be very clumsy, and approached the task of manipulating two delicate knitting needles and some thin wool with trepidation.

> 1   It is important to build on the student's previous experiences, both of practice and of learning. Any blocks to learning need to be identified (see Chapter 12), particularly ones which relate to the student's self-image: 'I'm clumsy.'

Questioning assumptions

It was rare for right-handed knitters to check whether the learner was left-handed, and left-handed learners were not aware that this was important. The few times when the learner was left-handed, the failure to check this out caused problems.

> 2   It is easy to make some basic assumptions which, if unchecked, can have difficult consequences. A student's reluctance to use a phone may be due to a hearing impairment rather than a lack of skill or confidence; it is a mutual responsibility to check this out, though the student does not always know what is relevant. Some differences are obvious, but others – like sexual preference, for example – are not.

Theory and practice

Although most learners have said that they benefit from a general overview, some said they would have preferred something detailed like a knitting pattern, while others said they were glad to be able to get stuck in straight away at a practical level, working piecemeal towards the larger picture.

> 3   Students have different styles of learning, so it is important not to assume the student will learn in the same ways as you do. It is useful to have different approaches available so that you can tune into the student's own learning wavelengths. However, as the placement progresses, the student should experiment with different learning styles. In knitting terms, it is useful to be flexible enough to follow a pattern and to be able to improvise as well.

Sequence of learning

It was common for the knitter to cast on stitches herself before teaching the learner the knit stitch. Casting on is considered more difficult than knitting, so the teacher often decided to start the learner off not with the first step (casting on) but with the easiest step (knit stitch). In those cases when the knitter started the learner at the very beginning, with the casting on stitch, the learner struggled and sometimes became frustrated.

> 4   It is easy to be tempted into thinking that sequences of learning should follow the same sequences as practice itself. However, practice may follow pattern ABCD, while learning might more naturally follow a different pattern – BCAD. How might patterns in social work learning differ from patterns in social work practice?

The power of demonstration

The opportunity to see teachers practising their art is essential. This provides credibility, and it allows teachers the opportunity to show what they mean. Try talking to somebody about how to knit without having access to needles or wool, and you will find it almost impossible to learn. All the learners found it useful to see the teacher knitting, though a few felt intimidated by very skilled knitters racing along the needle at great speed.

> 5   If knitting is near impossible to learn by talk alone, it is clear that a much more complex activity like social work is hollow without demonstration. For example, talking about interviewing skills is good preparation, but it is no substitute for the act of interviewing.
>
>   What benefits most students is a skilled rather than a superlative performance by the teacher; one which provides a good example, but not one which seems out of reach. The practice teacher has to learn how to break down a composite skill which has become second nature into one which can be explained carefully to a relative newcomer.

Hands-on

In many instances, knitter-teachers literally had their hands on the needles while the learners were using them. This tended to inspire learners with a lot of confidence, since it provided them with the most direct kind of feedback available and helped them feel safe that there was somebody 'to pick up the stitches'. However, on one occasion, a learner felt that having the knitter hold his hands while he was knitting was too controlling for his comfort.

> 6   It is important to develop a balance which lets the learner know that you are there, yet doesn't make the learner feel that they are 'watched' in an untrusting way. Guided practice, where practice teacher and student work together and the teacher is on hand to give direct feedback, is extremely valuable (see Evans, 1987). However, it is important to check that the hand is not too heavy, otherwise the student can feel over-controlled.

Anti-oppressive teaching

Of all the social divisions most evident in the *Knit one ...* activity, gender stands out clearly. In all but one of the groups where *Knit one ...* has been used, the knitter has been female and the learner male. In Western culture, by and large, *knitting = female*, though this has changed through the ages and is not true of all cultures presently. On one occasion, a male learner said he felt infantilized by the female teacher, who sat him on the floor in front of her so that she could position her hands on the needles from behind him. This differed from most hands-on teachers, who did this alongside the learner. The learner's response was probably as much about gender (men learning from women) as age.

7 The role of student and learner may not come easily. It may feel like a loss of power and status, or it may bring back unpleasant memories of school learning. Students need the opportunity to reflect on these, and to discuss the issue of power in the relationship with you (see Chapter 7). Discussing your respective learning styles is another opportunity to share differences and commonalities.

If knitting has different significance for different cultures at different times, do social work tasks also have a 'gender'?

Giving encouragement

The importance of encouragement to help the learner keep going, especially when it was difficult, was essential. Encouragement was expressed in a multitude of ways: verbal affirmation of the learner's progress, minimal encouragers (head nods, smiles, 'ahas', etc.), open body language, closeness, acknowledgement of the difficulty of the task, etc.

8 In Chapter 10, we described the importance of giving regular, affirming feedback. Especially when things are going badly, it is important that a general sense of encouragement is conveyed to build and maintain a 'climate for learning' (Knowles, 1983: 57–8).

Allowing mistakes

Learners frequently dropped stitches, and even the pair of needles, in their efforts to learn how to knit. Wool became tangled and wrongly threaded, and some strange-looking garments were on their way to being created. The novice knitters valued being allowed to make these mistakes and to learn from them.

9 The cliché, 'you learn by your mistakes', is a half-truth: you only learn if you have the chance to reflect on why it was a mistake, and an opportunity to rehearse and try again. The sequence of *practice–reflection–rehearsal–practice* can make good use of mistakes. Let students know that you expect them to make some mistakes, but that you also expect to help them to learn from them.

Avoiding jargon

Words which need some degree of specialist knowledge to understand them are jargon; even knitting is not spared its jargon. Learners found jargon words to be distracting and excluding. However, learners found short-hand terms like 'casting on' fine, after they had been explained and their meaning had come to life through the activity itself.

---

10   It is impossible to be completely jargon-free, because there are terms which are useful short-hand and which make communication between colleagues relatively rapid. Take care to introduce and explain short-hand terms only when they are really needed, and invite students to interrupt you to explain any word, phrase or acronym which they do not understand. We have all sat in meetings too embarrassed to ask what 'QWERTY' and the like means, so set an example for students by letting them see you asking colleagues to explain terms, too.

Valuing different practice styles

There seems to be a dominant methodology in the practice of knitting in the UK, though there have been a few notable variations in the *Knit one . . .* demonstrations. For instance, one knitter used a Continental practice of using only one needle. Observers who could knit were intrigued by different styles of knitting, since it challenged their assumption that 'everybody knits like I do'. Learners were not much interested in this expert talk and wanted to concentrate on the one method they had been taught.

---

11   The value of different social work practices should be respected, and it is useful for practice teachers to see other methods. However, there is probably limited value in exposing students to different social work methods before they feel skilled in one particular kind. The style of learning may well be influenced by the style of practice method, though we can only speculate about this in the absence of more research.

Each of these eleven aspects make up the general *climate for learning* which your student experiences on placement with you.

The practice teaching portfolio

Your portfolio should demonstrate evidence of how you helped to establish a climate for learning for a student, and you may wish to make reference to the issues described on pages 84–8, arising out of the *Knit one . . .* activity.

Example 11

Marion completed the learning styles questionnaire (Honey and Mumford, 1986) and found that her Theorist and Reflector scores were a lot higher than her scores for Pragmatist and Activist. This confirmed the impressions of Yasmin, her practice teacher, that she was someone who was meticulous and well-organized, and enjoyed conceptualizing her practice and careful planning before taking any action.

The previous student, June, had also completed the learning styles questionnaire, and her profile had been very different from Marion's. She scored high in the Activist and Pragmatist areas, but relatively low as a Theorist and a Reflector.

Yasmin described in her portfolio how she responded to these differences between Marion and June as learners – for example, how she adapted a particular exercise to suit their different learning styles. She commented on how she helped Marion and June to develop those learning styles which did not come naturally to them.

---

12 Blocks to learning

About Activity 12   The wall

The wall is a metaphor for the structures which might support and protect the student's learning or, alternatively, might build a barrier between students and their learning potential.

Purpose

We all create mental maps of the world to make sense of it, but sometimes we get stuck with these maps, unable to move on. Your concern as a practice teacher is not just what students learn, but *how* they learn, and how they learn to learn. This activity leads on to a consideration of blocks and barriers to learning and how to help students to develop flexible patterns of learning.

Method

- Think of a particular student you have taught, or are teaching at present.
- Consider each brick in *The wall* on page 92 in relation to the student – is it a support or a barrier? How does *The wall* shape up overall?
- Are there any other bricks you would name and add to *The wall*?

Variations

In addition to supporting your own learning as a practice teacher, you can use *The wall* in direct work with a student, as a way of introducing the notion of blocks to learning.

Activity 12   The wall

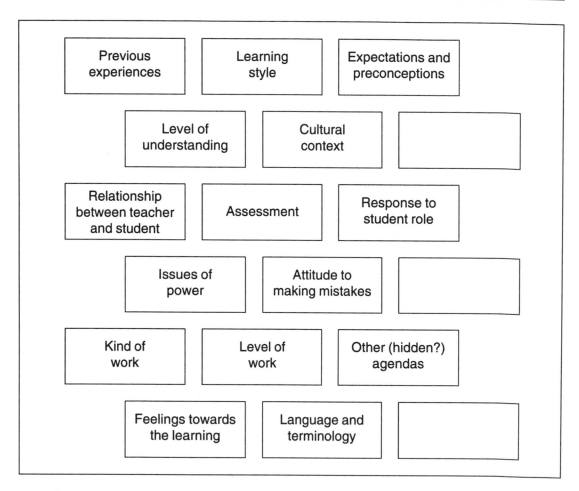

Walls can act as barriers or supports, or sometimes both at the same time – a Berlin Wall or the walls of your house. The bricks in the above wall can be *blocks to learning* or the *building blocks of learning*. Each brick is capable of acting in a helping or a hindering way, both in terms of the student's approach to learning and your own. Often it is the relationship between your teaching and the student's learning which is crucial – for example, do your expectations match each other's?

Consider each of the bricks in turn with respect to your work as a practice teacher with one or two particular students – did *The wall* become a support or a barrier? Or with potential students – how could *The wall* be a support or a barrier?

Notes for practice teachers

Participatory learning

Many adults in the UK are familiar with a style of teaching from their school days which was based on the empty vessel model; the pupil is there to be filled up with the accumulated knowledge of civilization. These kinds of experience can, in themselves, provide a block to the kind of teaching which emphasizes the learner's own powers of discovery and inquiry – the style apparent in this book, for example. Participatory learning may feel alien to somebody whose diet has been 'talk-and-chalk', and challenging because of the responsibility it places on the learner. If it is an excuse for lack of structure or preparation, it will feel aimless. Participatory learning does not mean having to invent everything yourself.

Brandes and Ginnis (1992: 11), writing for the school setting, contrast two approaches to teaching, which are variously called, on the one hand, 'student-centred', 'enquiry', 'experiential', 'participatory' and 'progressive', and on the other hand, 'subject-centred', 'formal', 'talk-and-chalk' and 'traditional'.

An adaptation of the contrast between these two approaches is shown below.

	Participatory	**Traditional**
1	teaching around integrated themes	teaching around discrete topics
2	teacher as a guide to educational experience	teacher as a distributor of knowledge and expertise
3	active student role; students participate in curriculum planning	passive student role; students have little or no say in curriculum planning
4	learning predominantly by discovery techniques	accent on memory, practice and rote
5	external rewards and sanctions not necessary, i.e. intrinsic motivation	external rewards used, such as grades, i.e. extrinsic motivation
6	not too concerned with conventional academic standards; little testing	emphasis on academic standards; regular testing
7	accent on cooperative groupwork	accent on competition
8	emphasis on creative expression; process valued	little emphasis on creative expression or process
9	cognitive and affective learning given equal emphasis	cognitive learning is emphasized; affective learning is not valued

There can be a tendency among teachers committed to participatory learning to throw the baby out with the bathwater. You might feel that there are aspects of the traditional approach which are worth preserving, or which are unavoidable, such as the need for 'testing' to make sure that clients are going to receive a good service. Learning to do social work is not like attending an adult education class in flower arranging, because of the powers which a social work qualification gives to its holder.

Your own experiences as a learner help to shape your outlook now. What kinds of learning experience have you had – as a pupil at school, as a student on placement? Can you identify your own blocks to learning?

Blocks to learning

Megginson and Boydell (1979: 15–16) identify four categories of blocks to learning and give examples of how these can be illustrated for training purposes:

- perceptual blocks (e.g. not being able 'to see the wood for the trees')
- cultural blocks (e.g. a deferential belief that the expert is always right)
- emotional blocks (e.g. fear of taking risks or 'looking silly')
- intellectual blocks (e.g. a difficulty with conceptualizing or handling ideas)

Blocks to learning occur at the organizational as well as the individual level. The climate for learning can be jeopardized not just by the personal blocks which Megginson and Boydell identify, but also by agency blocks. Senge (1990: 18–25) describes these as an organization's 'learning disabilities'. For example:

'I am my position'

The agency does not enable its employees to see beyond the boundaries of their own jobs, so there is duplication, conflict and a lack of overall purpose, and a tendency to blame other parts of the organization, or other agencies, when things go wrong.

The fixation on short-term events

Learning cannot be sustained if the organization is dominated by short-term outcomes and neglects longer-term processes. The parable of the boiled frog illustrates this:

> A frog dropped into a pan of boiling water will save itself by jumping out immediately. However, dropped into a pan of warming water, the frog will stay put, enjoying the warmth, becoming groggier and groggier until it no longer has the energy or will to escape, and then it is too late. The frog's survival reflexes are geared to sudden changes in its environment, not to gradual ones.
>
> (Summarized from Senge, 1990: 22–3)

Organizations are the same; it is not sudden change but slow change which can be the most destructive to the learning climate – and the survival – of an agency. Senge warns us to pay attention to the subtle changes as well as the dramatic events.

The delusion of learning from experience

There is a core learning dilemma: 'we learn best from experience but we never directly experience the consequences of many of our most important decisions' (Senge, 1990: 23). Trial and error learning is often not available, because the consequences of our actions are beyond our *learning horizons*. This is a vital consideration for practice learning, and leads us to the significance of simulations for learning (see Chapter 17).

The myth of the team

'When was the last time someone was rewarded in your organization for raising difficulty questions about the [agency's] current policies rather than solving urgent problems?' asks Senge (1990: 25). We are seldom given the space or freedom to appear uncertain, which in itself blocks new understandings and collective inquiry amongst colleagues. This leads to 'skilled incompetence' – teams of people who are very proficient at keeping themselves from learning.

What to do about these organizational learning blocks? A first step is to identify your agency's learning disabilities. As we saw in Chapter 8 (page 57), the practice context has a significant impact on the student's learning and your effectiveness as a practice teacher. You are not responsible for your agency's learning disabilities, but the student will rightly expect you to be aware of these, so they can be taken into account when weighing opportunities for learning.

Barriers to learning

In addition to blocks to learning, there are also barriers. Whereas blocks tend to be personal, barriers are cultural and structural (see Chapter 7). Some of the blocks identified in the previous section might be described as barriers, since they operate at a level which goes beyond the personal. An example of a barrier is the way the structure of a learning programme might exclude people who cannot commit themselves full-time; by reinforcing disadvantage and keeping out-groups out, barriers are powerful agents of structural oppression.

In a handy book designed to help people to teach themselves with open learning, Rowntree (1991: 23–5) identifies these common barriers to learning in traditional settings:

- lack of information
- unsuitable content
- unsuitable methods
- the qualifications gap
- timing, place and costs
- anxiety
- domestic pressures
- physical disabilities

One of these is more a block than a barrier – can you spot it?

Open learning programmes help some people to jump these barriers, by making the learning more flexible and accessible to a broader range of people. Does the placement which you can provide erect any barriers to learning – for instance, could a student in a wheelchair use your placement?

Patterns

Blocks to learning are not like blocks to plumbing: force and pressure will not relieve them. Finding out the nature of the block means helping students to identify patterns in their approach to learning.

The student might be relying on patterns which are no longer effective, or might not have the flexibility to change these patterns in response to different circumstances. Metaphors can reframe a situation in a powerful way, helping the student to get around a block to learning. Cunningham (1987: 52–5) uses a map as a metaphor to illustrate the way we make a coherent mental pattern of the world for ourselves. These internal maps need to be flexible enough to incorporate changes in the landscape, so that new developments (the 'motorways' and 'new towns' of the social world) are included. Sometimes it might be necessary to create a new map to meet different situations (e.g. if you wanted to find out about population density, a road map would be of limited use). Learning how these mental maps are created is essential to developing the flexibility to change patterns – learning how to learn.

Finally, it is important to acknowledge that learning involves a degree of 'quandary, query and qualms' (Snell, 1987: 62). The predominant messages about learning in this book are positive ones – that it is challenging, exciting and creative. However, it is also true that learning involves discomfort and de-skilling. Frequently it involves some unlearning, giving rise to emotions which are difficult for competent, coping adults to manage.

These patterns actually govern the way we see as well as how we think. Why does one person see a young woman in a hat and another see an old lady with a scarf in the picture below, and how long does it take for you to be able to see both? Once you are aware of both of the pictures, you can make a conscious decision to switch from one to the other.

(Taken from the 1987 *Annual Handbook for Group Facilitators*)

The practice teaching portfolio

Include in your portfolio any 'walls' you have analysed with respect to a student you have taught, and whether the bricks constituted a barrier or a support (page 92). Do you have any examples of work with students where there were blocks to learning, and, if so, how did you help the student to change their learning patterns?

Can you include in your portfolio an example of a participatory method and a traditional method of teaching you used with a student?

Example 12

Megan was a conscientious student who worked well with the residents in the home for older people where she was on placement with Sam. Although she was quiet and introverted, she was very skilled in individual work with the residents and was liked by them and by staff.

Despite the positive feedback which Megan received from Sam and others in the home, her poor image of her own abilities meant that she underestimated herself, and she avoided taking risks. Sam soon noticed a pattern of her avoiding situations where she would need to speak out or assert herself, and there was one member of the care staff who particularly intimidated her. Megan's mental map of herself did not square with the abilities Sam could see. In addition to the emotional block about taking risks, she had a cultural block which made her overly deferential to what she saw as the expertise of older staff.

Sam described in his portfolio how he helped Megan to identify her blocks to learning, what he did to help her overcome them, and whether he and she felt this was successful.

At the end of the placement, when Sam asked Megan if there was anything she felt she would have changed about her placement, she said that she wished that Sam had *made* her use video feedback (he had *suggested* using it to help develop Megan's assertiveness skills). Sam described the effect this had on his own learning as a practice teacher.

Module 5

Content of Practice Teaching

13 Knowledge, values, skills

About Activity 13   Menu

Menu is designed to start you naming all the different aspects of social work practice which you think a social work practitioner needs to know, be and do.

Purpose

The content of a curriculum is based on what a social work student needs to learn in order to do the job of social work. This is often viewed as a trinity of *knowledge, values* and *skills*, of which some will be general to all social workers, and some might be considered specialist. The curriculum should provide an integration of class-based learning and agency-based learning; as a practice teacher, your prime concern is the learning which takes place in the agency.

This activity asks you to think about what should be included in a curriculum for agency-based learning.

Method

- Get a large, blank sheet of flip-chart paper.
- Brainstorm all the components which you think the student should learn (don't try to categorize these components or make any judgements about them at this stage).
- On a second sheet of flip-chart paper, separate the items into three columns – 'knowledge', 'values' and 'skills'. You may want to put some items into more than one category.
- Compare your findings with CCETSW's *Requirements and Regulations for the Diploma in Social Work* (1991b: 14–17), and the Core Competencies in the *Review of Paper 30* (CCETSW, 1995).

Variations

Menu is more fun if you can arrange for a small group of practice teachers to work together. It is particularly helpful to include people who come from different settings or agencies, so that a variety of perspectives can be represented.

Activity 13   Menu

Get a large blank sheet of flip-chart paper, and brainstorm all the components of practice which you think the student should learn.

On a second sheet of paper, separate these items into three columns, 'knowledge', 'values' and 'skills'. Some items may appear in more than one column.

Example from a probation setting

What should the student learn on placement?

Knowledge	*Values*	*Skills*
• overview of the probation function	• use of authority	• report writing
• role of agency	• care and control	• liaison skills
• agency structure and admin	• anti-discriminatory practice	• court work
• role of professional	• ethical dilemmas	• time management
• guidelines on child protection	• issues of confidentiality	• strategy for planning for probation orders
• tariff issues	• awareness of own feelings	• evaluation skills
• throughcare	• self-presentation	• assessment skills
• law and sentencing	• openness and honesty	• coping with pressure
• working with sex offenders	• professional boundaries	• using supervision effectively
• court work		• interviewing skills
• Children Act		• groupwork skills
• duty work		• handling breach
		• decision making
		• duty work

These items were the results of a brainstorm with Probation Officers in 1992. The three categories were added after the brainstorm; most items are not exclusive to the category in which they are placed.

How do your lists compare with the Core Competencies and Practice Requirements in CCETSW's *Review of Paper 30* (1995)?

Notes for practice teachers

What is a curriculum?

Notions of curriculum have been commonplace in college-based learning but have only recently gained general currency in agency-based learning. 'Curriculum' is not a particularly friendly word, especially in view of its association in the UK with the political controversy of the national curriculum in schools. In these circumstances, it is important to make the idea of curriculum a friendly concept which will aid your practice teaching rather than hinder it (Doel, 1988: 45).

Elements of a curriculum

At the centre of a curriculum is the syllabus, which consists of four elements:

- the content of the learning
- the methods used to promote the learning
- the sequence and position of learning opportunities
- the assessment of the learning

In a sense, these are the 'what', 'how', 'when and where' and 'whether'.

The core value of a curriculum is that it provides a map for the student's learning. It is an explicit statement of expectations, some of which are negotiable and some of which are not. In the field of practice learning, some aspects of a curriculum may be difficult to control, such as the timing of learning opportunities; the careful mix of learning from planned, timed simulations and learning from live activities is part of the art, science and technology of practice teaching. The question of sequence should not be abandoned because of the challenges of the practice learning environment (Doel, 1990). However, the term 'sequence' is linear, and it needs to be supplemented with the notion of 'position' – like pieces in a jigsaw puzzle.

The syllabus of contents, methods, sequences and assessment is transformed into a true curriculum by two overarching features. First, what are the *aims* of the curriculum, and who defines those aims? In part, CCETSW has outlined the curriculum in its *Requirements and Regulations for the Diploma in Social Work* (1991b) and subsequent *Review* (CCETSW, 1995), but greater definition has to be provided by local programmes. The second feature is the *evaluation* of the curriculum. How are the various elements of the syllabus to be evaluated to ensure that the aims are being met, and how are the results of this evaluation to be fed back into the elements of the curriculum?

Negotiated learning

A curriculum is not effective if it feels like a straitjacket. It should provide form and framework to your work with the student, not a rigid set of directions – it should be a map which allows you to *choose* the highway or the byway. The student will be expected to demonstrate specific results, but the routes to those outcomes will be varied. Translating the general curriculum into specific content for your setting and with particular meaning for each individual student is a practice teaching skill.

Different routes to a practice curriculum

There are a number of different routes which can be used to begin to construct a curriculum for practice learning. Doel (1988) has identified three:

The paradigm route

One way to construct a practice curriculum is to design a comprehensive blueprint of social work practice. For example, CCETSW Paper 20.6 (1986) offers a matrix of methods, contexts and client groups along the divisions of groupwork, casework and community social work.

Butler and Elliott (1985) construct a comprehensive paradigm of five skill areas, twelve basic life situations and four contexts of practice, to form a matrix of possible combinations:

Skill areas	**Basic life situations**
● thinking skills	● beginnings
● feeling skills	● dependency
● communication skills	● ambivalence
● processing work through time	● conflict
● learning skills	● group contact
	● unhappiness in relations
Contexts of practice	● deficiencies
	● crisis
● self	● achievement
● one or two others	● illness
● groups and communities	● deterioration
● agencies and organizations	● endings and loss

In order to avoid the student having to show competence in each of the 240 cells in their matrix, Butler and Elliott emphasize the need to transfer and translate learning from one experience to another. Nevertheless, the blueprint is complex, and looks like a tall order for both practice teacher and student.

The broad framework

A second route is the broadbrush approach, in which the curriculum illustrates general areas of social work practice.

Margaret Richards (1988) offers a good example in her reframing of the matrix in CCETSW Paper 20.6 (1986). She describes three levels of work, called 'primary', 'secondary' and 'tertiary', emphasizing that this is not a hierarchy: 'Each sphere has its own knowledge, skills and complexities. Each needs to be understood and valued by social workers, though not necessarily practised by all in their subsequent employment' (Richards, 1988: 11).

The *primary sphere* revolves around a philosophy of developing the competencies of people whose failure to obtain resources or to influence political discussion means that their basic needs are not being met. The work is characterized by consumer participation, openness of communication and the concept of mutuality; fundamental to success is the capacity to 'work alongside' the people the student is helping.

Control is often at the heart of the *secondary sphere*, with the student walking a tightrope between the needs of the named client and close others. Work in this sphere is with people who are unable to manage crucial social work roles, such as 'good-enough parenting'. The power of the worker – whether fulfilling a statutory role or as guardian of scarce resources – is a fundamental element in this sphere of work. A certain amount of role distance and detailed specialist knowledge is necessary.

In the *tertiary sphere*, the worker must meet the needs of people requiring 24-hour coverage, in whatever setting. The threat to independent living is high, and the task for the student is how to maintain the person's sense of identity and self-esteem. This might be in the form of direct help to the client (in residential care, for instance) or in indirect help to carers. Role intimacy and a capacity to deal with the stress this can cause is necessary to success.

Richards (1988: 15) suggests that students would be expected to show a basic competence in all three spheres, but aim to 'major' only in two. She also recommends a Foundation Unit to provide students with an overview of the full range of social work and a base line of competence, providing some credits, *before* full training in practical work begins.

The empirical approach

A third approach is to reconstruct a curriculum based on what is considered to be the best of existing practice. There always has been a curriculum of sorts, and the task of the curriculum-builder is to inspect the implicit and unsystematic curriculum and reframe it so that it is explicit and systematic; take the parts that 'work' and make them work better.

The practice curriculum developed by Doel (1987b) is an example of this approach. Six modules outline 'clusters' of learning, with attention to methods and sequence of learning as well as content. The modules in the first curriculum were designed for three periods of practice learning:

- Period 1
  - working in the agency (the skills of personal organization)
  - initial skills (the skills of engaging others)
- Period 2
  - social work methods (the skills of helping others over time)
  - work with different users (the skills of generic practice)
- Period 3
  - working on the agency (the skills of influencing others)
  - working with and in groups (the skills of working with many others)

The curriculum below illustrates a modular approach applied to the first placement of the Diploma in Social Work (South Yorkshire, 1993). It outlines three main areas of practice learning – *modules* – each of which is divided into smaller clusters of learning – *units*. The first unit starts with the student, and looks out at the work through her or his eyes. It helps students and practice teachers to articulate their beliefs and values, alongside each other.

The second module, is concerned with the student's skills in direct work with people who use the agency's services. Students develop their interpersonal skills and planning abilities to bring purpose into their direct contacts, and to work systematically with people over time. There are beginnings, middles and ends to planned pieces of work with clients.

In the third module, the student is expected to look through the agency's eyes, learning to cultivate good professional practice in the daily reality of a social work agency. The emphasis is not just on individual professionalism, but on how to be a team member and how to make links with other agencies and work in an interdisciplinary way.

This first placement gives the student a grounding in social work practice, ready for further class-based learning and a second placement in a focused area of practice, where learning is associated with a particular client group or practice setting.

Module 1	**Values in action**
Unit 1.1	Orientation
Unit 1.2	Practice philosophy
Unit 1.3	Power and oppression
Unit 1.4	Anti-racist practice
Unit 1.5	Professional boundaries
Unit 1.6	Self-presentation
Module 2	**Direct work with people**
Unit 2.1	Communication skills

continued

Unit 2.2	Preparation for direct work
Unit 2.3	Beginnings (exploring problems)
Unit 2.4	Middles (work on problems)
Unit 2.5	Endings (reviewing work)
Unit 2.6	Selecting a practice method

Module 3   Managing the work

Unit 3.1	Time management
Unit 3.2	Workload management
Unit 3.3	Managing the resources
Unit 3.4	Skills in recording
Unit 3.5	Working in a team
Unit 3.6	Working with other agencies

(*Source:* South Yorkshire, 1993)

It is the responsibility of the *programme* to create a curriculum for practice learning, not *yours* as the individual practice teacher. You need to be aware both of the details of the student's curriculum and the general philosophy which underpins it, in order to use it and to evaluate its effectiveness. Your understanding of the curriculum is the first step towards making appropriate learning opportunities available for the student.

The practice teaching portfolio

What goes into your portfolio in this section is very much influenced by the nature of the practice curriculum for the student's Diploma in Social Work programme. If you have a clearly organized curriculum for the placement, you will need to demonstrate how you relate this to your particular setting. However, if there is no common practice curriculum, you may have to take more individual responsibility for developing one.

Some programmes rely on 'free-standing' competencies to direct the student's learning (in other words, they are not clustered into modules) and these can look overwhelming (see Chapter 20). A list of competencies is not a practice curriculum, since it does not provide all four pillars of a curriculum as described on page 103.

Example 13

Gurnam is a practice teacher in a voluntary organization which works with children and families. The agency is in the middle of a large council estate with a very high unemployment rate; in addition to social divisions along race and gender lines, it is evident that poverty is a huge social division, oppressing many people who live on the estate.

In negotiation with Jim, the student on placement, Gurnam decided to supplement the local practice curriculum with a module of learning based on 'Poverty'. He felt that it was an important aspect of the social work practice in his locality, and that it needed the 'status' of its own module, rather than being fitted into others.

Gurnam included the unit on 'Poverty' in his portfolio, explaining the rationale for including it, and how he taught it. This unit formed the basis of his portfolio project, with some additional work about how he had evaluated the impact of this unit on the student's learning and practice.

14 Curriculum development

About Activity 14   Jigsaw

Jigsaw is a way of thinking about what you do as a practitioner and taking a step back to think about how you might teach what you do. It takes one small piece of practice – a part of the social work practice jigsaw – and prompts you to develop it into an opportunity for learning.

Purpose

Practice teachers are expected to use a practice curriculum which has become more explicit and systematic. The task of developing a comprehensive curriculum is one for the programme as a whole, not the individual practice teacher, but you will need to think about how the curriculum relates to your own practice. This module helps you to understand how learning objectives relate to actual practice.

Method

- Review the notes on page 103 of Chapter 13.
- Take a specific piece of practice from your own recent work and note it down (there are two example pieces at the top of page 111).
- Use the questions in the *Jigsaw* piece on page 110 to transform your piece of practice into a piece of curriculum.
- Later, see how this piece relates to the curriculum for your local Diploma in Social Work programme. (If it is modular, which modules or units does it refer to?)

Variations

Jigsaw uses the empirical approach to developing a curriculum (pages 105–7). You might want to try another route – for example, the broadbrush approach. Relate your piece of practice to the spheres of practice which Richards (1988) describes in her two-part article, summarized on pages 104–5.

Activity 14   Jigsaw

Looking back on your work over the last week or so, select a particular piece of practice which you feel it is important for a student to learn about. It should be a specific situation, and it does not have to be a glowing piece of good practice. (The two examples at the top of page 111 are given as a rough guide.)

Taking this piece as one small part of the overall picture of social work practice, consider how you would teach it, using the questions in the jigsaw piece as a guide.

Content

How would you describe the content of the learning?
Describe this in three or four learning objectives which the student would be expected to achieve in connection with this piece of practice.

Methods

How might the student learn about this piece of practice?
Brainstorm three or four ways in which you might teach the student and make a brief note of the advantages and disadvantages of each.

Position

How does this jigsaw piece fit with other aspects of practice?
Are there any other pieces of learning which should be in place before the student is introduced to this particular piece of practice?

Assessment

How do you know whether and when the student has achieved the learning objectives for this piece of practice?
What indicators would demonstrate to other people that the student had been successful?
Develop 3 or 4 indicators for one of the learning objectives.

Example pieces of the jigsaw of practice

Mrs Paley was very upset when I saw her on Tuesday. She was feeling depressed about whether she would ever be in a position to look after her own children again, and she burst into tears in the middle of it all. She seemed very lonely and vulnerable and in need of a cuddle. She said she wished *she* could be taken into care.

I hadn't expected the meeting to be so hostile to the idea of Mr Badhuri coming into the Unit. I felt that he would get a lot from what we could offer, and that he wanted to give it a try, but only Janice seemed to be with me. I felt I hadn't done him justice, and I wondered whether issues of race and gender were getting in the way of us making a proper decision.

Notes for practice teachers

An explicit practice curriculum should describe each piece in the practice jigsaw puzzle in enough detail for you to know what it means, but not so much that you are unable to translate it to your own particular setting.

The example module below is taken from Module 1, 'Values in Action', of a Placement One Curriculum which consists of eighteen units of learning (South Yorkshire, 1993).

Consider what each learning objective means in the context of your own practice.

Example unit: Professional boundaries

Description

This unit focuses on the student's ability to understand the differences between friendships and professional relationships ('workships'), and to recognize their own power and authority in relation to different groups.

Learning objectives

The student should demonstrate an ability to:

1 Develop self-awareness of their own style of making working relationships.
2 Understand the differences between informal and formal relationships and the function of professional distance and boundaries.
3 Use different styles in making relationships, appropriate to the work.
4 Exercise professional authority when necessary whilst recognizing the power imbalance introduced by gender, culture, age, race, disability, etc.
5 Refrain from using professional authority automatically.
6 Explore with clients the issues involved when client and worker share similar experiences of oppression (e.g. black workers with black clients, women with women, disabled with disabled, etc.).[1]

---

[1] Doel and Shardlow (1993: 23–4) have an activity to trigger teaching and learning for this unit.

Links with the college-based curriculum

We have been exploring the jigsaw of social work practice and the different 'pieces' which complete this picture. However, this is only a part of the picture. The overall curriculum for the student social worker includes periods of class-based learning in the college as well as periods of practice-based learning in the agency. How do the large jigsaws of agency and college fit together?

Sawdon (1986: 61) has described how easily these two aspects of student learning can splinter, and the possible collusion of college tutors and of practice teachers with students' criticisms of the other 'side'. There is a tension which is perhaps unavoidable between these two locations of learning, because their primary functions (education and social service provision) are so different.

The curriculum has the potential to bridge the college–agency gap. It can help both 'sides' win, which is a gain for both the student and social work's clients:

- *The notion of curriculum provides a framework which is common to both places of learning.* Students benefit if they experience a common language in both locations of learning. The language of the curriculum provides a shared conceptual framework, which is important for mutual understanding.
- *The practice curriculum is empowering for practice teachers and students.* The concept of curriculum originated in the college setting, but its adaptation to the agency setting empowers practice teachers by asserting the educational aspects of their work with students (often undervalued), and its explicitness demonstrates the full extent of the practice teaching task to agency managers. It has the potential to empower students because it presents them with something specific to work with and negotiate about; something open to challenge.
- *The practice curriculum enables people who are not directly involved in the teaching to understand what is being taught.* An explicit curriculum lets college-based and agency-based teachers know what each other are doing. This opens up the opportunity to review the whole curriculum together, to see how it is meeting the needs of individual students and whether the aims of the programme are being achieved.
- *The practice curriculum begins to make demands on the college curriculum.* Placements should no longer be seen as testing grounds for what is learned in college. This approach was sometimes referred to as 'putting it into practice', and the 'it' was invariably what was learned in college. The practice curriculum brings the 'it' into the agency-based learning, perhaps as a prerequisite of class learning, and able to influence the content of the class curriculum – a practice-led curriculum (Phillipson et al., 1988). Some programmes have a period of practice learning at the start of the programme, before the class-based work.

As a practice teacher, you need to gain some familiarity with the college curriculum, just as the tutor should be familiar with the practice curriculum. This does not have to be detailed, but enough to help you understand how the student's learning on placement dovetails with their learning in class. Students also need to take responsibility for making these connections.

Organization of the class curriculum

Just as there are many ways in which the practice curriculum might be developed (see pages 104–6), so the organization of the class-based curriculum varies from one programme to another.

Haines (1985: 124–33) outlines ten alternatives:

- *Core* Core content has to be followed by all students on the programme. Apart from the difficulties of identifying what is core, and the resultant expansion of the curriculum content, few courses in any subject involve *only* core teaching. Even if the principle of core teaching is accepted, it will be combined with something else to guarantee flexibility.
- *Core plus options or electives* A smaller core gives students more options to match their interests. Some electives may be core for some students, but optional for others (e.g. working with offenders would be compulsory for probation students, but not others). There is always difficulty in deciding what should be core and what should be optional, such as teaching about group-work, because of the sense that 'optional' means 'less important'.
- *Generic/specific* This approach might provide a generic base on which specific teaching may be built. Unitary or integrated methods might be offered as the generic core, emphasizing common principles and foundation skills. Haines (1985: 125) wonders whether it might be possible to invert this process and start from the specific before moving to the general, and suggests that there is likely to be a constant interchange between the two. Students have different learning styles: some learn more easily by starting with the generic, and others by starting with the specific (see Chapter 11).
- *Generalist/specialist* Similar to the previous approach, except that the general base is linked to a degree of specialization in the curriculum (whether by method, client group or setting). These are sometimes called *concentrations*; students would receive some general grounding in a subject like community work, but would have a choice about whether to go further in that subject later.

The following approaches are not so well established as the previous ones:

- *Theme-centred, problem-based* Teaching is focused on particular themes, such as poverty, loss, the family, etc. These themes cross social work theories and methods, client groups, contexts, etc., and often involve interdisciplinary teaching. They may use student-led groups for much of the active learning. An example is the Enquiry and Action Learning approach at Bristol University (Burgess, 1992).
- *Macro/micro* Themes are viewed as a sequence which moves from a broad, societal perspective, via communities, groups and families, to the individual (the reverse is possible, too).
- *Life stages* The curriculum follows the sequence of the stages in a life cycle, using a particular theoretical base. Students learn about social work practice through the characteristics, problems and strengths of each phase.

- *Modular approaches*   Clusters of learning are identified as discrete portions or modules. Students in distance or open learning programmes can follow a modular programme at their own pace, building credits which build incrementally towards the Diploma in Social Work. Haines (1985: 127) comments that, 'unless it can be demonstrated that there is something about training for social work that requires two years of continuous study and practice overseen and supported by personal tutors and practice teachers,' this is a feasible system.
- *Individualized – student/tutor choice*   Each individual student constructs a learning contract with a personal tutor which is tailored to the particular learning needs of the student. 'It can be carried to the point where there is virtually no formal, written syllabus' (Haines, 1985: 127).
- *Integrated*   Difficult to define because 'it is like having to draw an animal you have never seen from a written description of its features' (Haines, 1985: 127). The integrated approach focuses on the coherence of theory and practice, the transfer of learning and, of course, it seeks to integrate agency-based and college-based learning.

Contracting with specific training programmes

It is difficult for a practice teacher to get to grips with the course philosophy, the curriculum design and the placement pattern of a DipSW programme; it is nearly impossible to do this with a number of programmes. For this reason, the notion of contractual arrangements with one particular programme is becoming more attractive. This can be an agency-wide agreement or at individual practice teacher level, and it means you contracting with a particular programme, perhaps to take a student for a specific placement on a regular basis. It helps you to feel a part of a teaching team as you become more familiar with the particular programme, and the programme gets to know your placement profile and the particular learning opportunities you have to offer (see Chapter 4).

The practice teaching portfolio

You might want to include in your portfolio any 'jigsaw pieces' you have been working on, in order to develop your own interpretation of the programme's practice curriculum. Either way, you should include specific examples in your portfolio which show how you have translated some of the learning objectives into practice with a specific student.

Example 14

Rosa is a practice teacher working in a Probation Service. Following a recent episode with an aggressive client, she was especially aware of the importance of learning how to deal with aggression.

Familiarity with the agency's relevant policy document was one of the learning objectives for this piece of practice, but also included were interpersonal skills and interviewing strategies. Rosa decided to use the 'what if?' method, posing questions to the student which added hypothetical developments to the student's actual work with clients. This related very well to teaching other interpersonal skills, especially observation of non-verbal communication.

In her portfolio, Rosa described the teaching of this particular piece of practice, and how she related it to the practice curriculum. The student was not faced with an aggressive situation where she had to put the learning into direct practice, but Rosa noted occasions when the student was using the knowledge gained from their discussions to manage difficult situations.

15 Theory and practice

About Activity 15   In theory ... In practice

In theory ... In practice is one example of how to teach students to think about the ways in which theories underpin practice and practice informs theory. It may trigger other kinds of activity for you to develop in your practice teaching.

Purpose

'Integration of theory and practice' has been a pious hope in many a course handbook. Unfortunately, there has been little guidance for the practice teacher to put this good intention to work. This chapter recognizes the importance of this aspect of the practice curriculum by helping you to consider how to teach the integration of theory and practice; it also considers how you might integrate practice teaching theory and practice.

Method

Before asking the student to complete *In theory ... In practice*, you should complete your own examples, so you are familiar with the task you have set the student.

- Take each part – *In theory* and *In practice* – in turn (it is helpful, but not essential, to consider them in the same session).
- Make sure you return to this activity at some point later in the placement, to see how the student has made use of her or his learning. You should also consider the extent to which you have integrated theory and practice in your own practice teaching.

Variations

If you want to gain a variety of perspectives, or to consider one theory in relation to different practice settings, it is useful to use this activity in a small group of practice teachers (with or without student participation).

Activity 15(1)   In theory

Together with the student, focus on one theoretical perspective which contributes to social work (you can pitch this at a grand theory level, such as one of the feminist perspectives described in Chapter 3 of Rojek et al. (1988), or at the level of practice method, such as Transactional Analysis theory). You and the student do not have to be in sympathy with the theory.

Take two or three pieces of social work practice from the student's experiences in the agency during the previous week. These should involve specific, direct contacts with residents, clients or communities, but could also include meetings, agency policies, etc. Consider each of these in the light of the particular theory you have decided to use.

How can you use this activity to teach the student how this theory might influence what they would do?

Activity 15(2)   In practice

Ask the student to collect a piece of practice. This should concern a resident, client or community group, either as a piece of direct work, or work on behalf of the resident, client or community group.

The student should give a brief description of what happened; not a detailed or lengthy case history, but an accurate observation of events, without evaluation at this stage. This, in itself, is a useful skill for the student to develop.

Together with the student, use these headings to consider how the experience of this particular piece of practice might inform different kinds of theory:

- *Grand Theory* (e.g. Marxist theories of class conflict)
- *Theories of Social Policy* (e.g. social attitudes to lone parents)
- *Theories of Practice Method* (e.g. the stages of group formation in groupwork)
- *Practice Wisdom* (e.g. a generally held belief that you should not challenge the delusions of older, confused people)

How did the student experience the difference between starting from a theoretical perspective, as with *In theory*, from starting from a piece of practice, as with *In practice*?

Notes for practice teachers

One of the key tasks of a practice teacher is to enable a student to put theory into practice – or is it about putting practice into theory? 'Integrating theory and practice' is one of the more difficult aspects of the student's curriculum, not least because of the historical association which too frequently links theory to what is learned in colleges, and practice to what is done in agencies.

It is also an area where practitioners often feel 'rusty' and uncertain of where the line between class-based and practice-based learning should be drawn. This chapter is designed to demystify theory, and to help practice teachers feel confident about integrating it into their teaching.

There are three critical questions which practice teachers need to address from the start: What do we mean by 'theory?' How can theory and practice be integrated? Where should theory be taught?

What do we mean by 'theory'?

It helps to acknowledge that there are different kinds of theory. In *Modern Social Work Theory*, Payne (1991: 52) distinguishes four types:

- 'theories *about* social work explain the nature and role of social work in society'
- 'theories *of* social work describe which activities constitute social work, set aims for social work activities and explain why those activities are relevant and effective in meeting the aims'
- 'theories *contributing* to social work are the psychological, sociological and other theories which explain or describe personal and social behaviour and are used to make theories of social work systematic, related to general social science explanations and to give supporting evidence for the social work theory's prescriptions'
- 'theories of social work *practice and method* prescribe in detail how the other theories so far outlined may be applied in the interaction between workers and clients'

In her *Handbook of Theory for Practice Teachers in Social Work*, Lishman (1991) distinguishes models of understanding human development from models of social work intervention. Examples of the former are Attachment Theory, Erikson's Life Cycles, and approaches such as Psychodynamic and Structural. Examples of the latter included in the book are behavioural social work, crisis intervention, task-centred practice, a cognitive-behavioural perspective, psychodynamic counselling, community social work and working within the life-space.

The student will find some theories more helpful in explaining things and increasing their understanding, whilst other theories will be more helpful in suggesting what to do and developing their skills.

How can theory and practice be integrated?

Payne (1991: 39–50) considers three debates about the difficulties in applying theory in practice. The first is a *pragmatic* argument that there are too many theories, and they are not practically useful because they are highly generalized and imported from other disciplines – in other words, they do not give clear-cut guidance about what to do in a specific situation. Payne suggests that this argument is actually 'a struggle for control of social work theory between different interests within social work'. The second debate is the *positivist* argument that social work theory is 'soft science', insufficiently rigorous, describing and hypothesizing rather than explaining. The third is the *eclecticism* debate, which suggests that it is possible and desirable to move between theories or to use parts of different theories in combination – for example, systems theories attempt to develop an overarching theory to include many or all other social work theories.

Barbour (1984) identified three models by which the social work students in her study understood the integration of theory with practice:

- *'seeping in'*, where students had acquired general ideas and methods but were unable to say where these had come from
- *'amalgam'*, where particular theories were used where they seemed relevant, and each student built up a stock of 'professional lore' to be used as required
- *'personal style'*, where knowledge was said to be integrated with the student's personality to form a seamless whole (quoted in Payne, 1991: 55)

Integrating theory and practice is an extremely difficult process. Evans (1992: 30) identifies five distinct abilities subsumed in the phrase 'applying theory to practice':

- to conceptualize key variables in a practice context
- to recognize the relevance of a theory
- to understand the theory
- to shape the theory for the practice context
- to recognize whether the theory thus shaped did in fact benefit the practice context

No small order, but one made more manageable if students are taught how to make explicit links between knowledge and action. The knowledge might be at the level of 'Grand Theory' or practice method.

Where should theory be taught?

The practice curriculum has made more demands of practice teachers to teach theories of social work practice and method (the fourth of Payne's types of theory; see page 119). Agency-based learning gives students the opportunity to observe practitioners using a practice method and to try it out for themselves. It provides the chance to explore different approaches to social work practice, and for students to think about the implicit theories by which they interpret the world (see Doel and Shardlow, 1993: 'Worldview', 13–20).

The student should also learn to become aware of the impact of practice wisdom or practice theory (see Curnock and Hardiker, 1979). Students are likely to find that untested assumptions and practice experience inform practice in agencies more than a coherent, systematic theory (this statement is, itself, an example of practice wisdom!). It is important for students to learn how to recognize practice wisdom, and to discuss it critically with their practice teachers.

There is one sense in which it is impossible not to teach some kind of theory in practice settings – actions which have any sense of direction at all must be based on knowledge, values and beliefs, even if these are not made explicit. There is perhaps nothing more dangerous than 'covert theory', and, if for no other reason than avoiding this danger, the reflective practitioner is one who is able to make these 'theories for action' explicit.

A theory of practice teaching

So far we have been discussing the content of the curriculum for practice learning; in other words, ways in which you might teach students to integrate different kinds of theory into their social work practice. As a practice teacher, you will also need to consider how you integrate theories relevant to practice teaching into your teaching. For example, how do you make use of theories which explain how adults learn? (See Chapters 10, 11, 12.)

Bogo and Vayda (1987: 1–9) discuss the theoretical base of field instruction (practice teaching). They describe Kolb's four-stage cycle of learning: (1) concrete experience is followed by (2) observation and reflection, which leads to (3) the formation of abstract concepts and generalizations, which leads to (4) hypotheses to be tested in future action, which in turn leads to new experience. Their adaptation of this learning cycle to social work education has produced the ITP (Integration of Theory and Practice) Loop which can be used at any level of social work intervention.

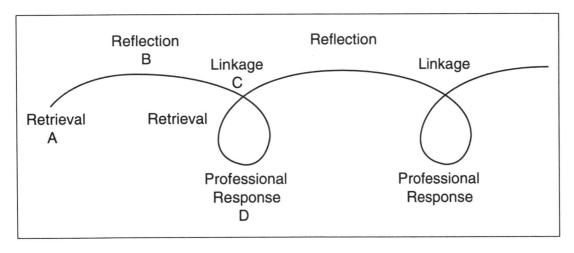

The loop is a way of:

- analysing how students observe the world: *A – retrieval of factual elements;*
- making sense of these 'facts': *B – reflecting on the way their observation is modified by their personal biography, and evaluating the effectiveness of the intervention;*
- then: *C – linking these processes to professional knowledge that can explain or account for the findings of the preceding steps;*
- leading to the choice of: *D – a professional response to the action or event that began the loop.*

This, in turn, begins the process of the next loop. In short, it helps the student to develop into a reflective practitioner, and it requires the practice teacher to make explicit those processes which might have become 'gut' or intuitive.

Bogo and Vayda suggest that practitioners often use the ITP Loop tacitly as part of their own practice wisdom, but that the reflection and linkage elements may be lost as practice competence becomes more routine. They emphasize that practice teachers should learn to use the loop themselves before teaching it to students.

Example unit: Selecting a practice method

Description

This unit develops the student's understanding and practice of working systematically over time with individuals or groups.

'What is not advisable is having no method at all and just "doing" social work (as if this can somehow not involve having a view of how people "tick" and what values are held).' (Coulshed, 1991: 5)

As a minimum, students should develop an understanding of different approaches to social work practice, and a detailed understanding of at least one social work practice method in a residential, day care or field setting. The student should have direct practice experience of using one practice method during this placement, even if this is not successfully completed.

Learning objectives

The student should demonstrate an ability to:

1   Understand what is meant by a practice method.
2   Show a beginner's knowledge of different approaches to social work practice, and how theories and values inform practice methods. This should include the opportunity to see other practitioners using different approaches or methods.
3   Use at least one particular method of social work practice, even if this is not successfully completed. This should include an understanding of its limitations as well as its applications.
4   Understand how this particular method is anti-oppressive and to use it in an anti-oppressive way.
5   Start to make judgements about the relative merits of different approaches (e.g. in promoting anti-oppressive practice; in being culturally relevant; in being effective, etc.).

Notes: See Coulshed (1991) and Hanvey and Philpot (1994) for different approaches to social work; Doel and Shardlow (1993: 47) outline a practice method, and a detailed example of one practice method in action is Doel and Marsh's (1992) *Task-Centred Social Work*.

Opposite is another piece of the social work jigsaw described in Chapter 14. This piece is concerned with the way the student works over time with people who are using the agency's services, and the development of expertise in a practice method. It is taken from the practice curriculum for Placement One – Module 2, 'Direct Work with People' (South Yorkshire, 1993).

Consider what each learning objective means in the context of your own practice.

The practice teaching portfolio

It is not necessary to show a comprehensive understanding of 'Grand Theory' in your portfolio. What *is* important, however, is to include evidence which demonstrates your ability as a reflective practice teacher. This means that you are able to move from:

observations of the student's practice

↓

making sense of these observations (includes reflecting on personal biographies)

↓

explaining your observations by linking them to your knowledge base

↓

choosing a response to address the observations which started this cycle

Example 15

Gaynor is a practice teacher in a community-based project. She described the way she used the ITP Loop (page 121) in connection with her practice teaching.

She had *observed* for some time that her student, Tim, had a tendency to dominate meetings of a community group which was set up to survey need on a large council estate. She held back to begin with, because she was aware of her own bias towards a facilitative style. However, when she *reflected* on the impact of Tim's style over a few meetings, her evaluation was that Tim was holding the group back, and that there was a danger that possible leaders within the group were feeling a loss of power.

She *linked* her experience and knowledge as a practice teacher with her direct knowledge of this particular student, Tim. She judged that a direct confrontation was unlikely to be successful, based on earlier observations of Tim becoming defensive when she had tried this approach. However, she believed that Tim genuinely valued the idea of empowerment.

She decided to *select a response* built on her understanding of adult learners as problem-solvers and self-motivated. This was particularly true of Tim. With his permission and the permission of the group, she videoed one of the meetings, and asked Tim to observe the tape as if he were one of the participants. She told him that she felt that there was a problem, but that she wanted his analysis of what was going on before she gave her account. Having seen the tape, Tim's criticisms of his own conduct at the meeting were so sharp, that Gaynor found it necessary to help him to look at his strengths and to focus on what changes he was going to make at the next community group meeting (continuing *reflection*).

She gave an account of this in her portfolio to illustrate the way she had used theory to develop her own practice teaching.

Module 6

Methods of Practice Teaching

16 The practice tutorial

About Activity 16   Action techniques

This activity helps you to consider the different methods you can use to help a student with a problem. *Action techniques* is taken from a handout developed by Catherine Sawdon and consists of five categories of practice teaching methods, plus a sixth category concerned with the structural arrangements for the teaching. How might you use elements from each different category to help the student's learning? Finally, you are asked to consider how you would tailor your choice of methods to an individual student.

Purpose

The practice tutorial, or supervision session, is central to the student's learning. It provides an opportunity for direct teaching, for rehearsal, reflection and assimilation. This chapter provides a critique of the traditional use of the supervision session and encourages you to broaden your repertoire of practice teaching methods, both inside and outside the practice tutorial.

Method

- Focus on a problem which the student has brought to the practice tutorial, or provide a simulated situation (such as the one on page 130).
- Consider each of the five categories of *Action techniques* in turn. Make a note of what you could do to help the student's learning in each category. Be specific.
- Consider the different structural arrangements for the teaching. How might they fit with the different methods?
- Make choices about which methods and arrangements you would use to help the student with the practice problem.
- Finally, consider how your knowledge of an individual student would influence your choice of methods (it helps to have one or two actual students in mind, but if you do not have this experience, consider a couple of your colleagues).

Variations

This activity works especially well in a group which can split into pairs or smaller groups (each looking at just one of the five categories). Start with a brief role-play to reproduce the situation in the practice tutorial – this helps to bring the student's problem to life and trigger ideas.

Activity 16   Action techniques

Take a problem which a student has brought to a practice tutorial. Consider each of the five categories below (taken from Sawdon, 1985), and make a note in each category of what you could do to help the student's learning in connection with the problem (an example is given).

1 Hardware

Audio   Video   Tape
Slide
Film   Computer
One-way screens
Internet   CD-TV
(Interactional video)

2 Written

Practice folder   Minutes
Logs   Reports   Summaries
Day books   Case records
Resource file   Task analysis
Questionnaires   Letters
Critical Incident Analysis
Contracts   Evaluation sheets
Individual care plans
Recorded, timed observations

3 Experiential

Exercises   Activities
Games   Role-play
Drama
Rehearsal   Simulations
Sculpting   'Quick-think'
Discussions   Meetings
Project development
Court appearances
Ward rounds   Tribunals

4 Graphic

OHP   Flip-charts   Plans
Photographs   Diagrams
Drawings   Cartoons
Sketches   Charts

Structural Arrangements

One-to-One   Tandem   Peer
Group   Pair(s)
Co-work   Joint work
Live teaching
Tag   Long-arm   Outreach
Periodic on-site
Observed   Direct evidence
Team   Linked

5 Printed

Articles   Handouts
Books   Novels
Texts   Reports
Newspaper items
Journals   Statistics
Official document analysis
Policy documents
Procedures manuals

Example

Ray is in the fifth week of his seventeen-week block placement with you. He has started a group for the carers of older, confused people, and after the first session, he is concerned that the only male member of the group, Frank, is dominating it. Ray is a conscientious, reflective student, but finds it hard to take the plunge and sometimes holds back. His main concern was his inability to confront Frank over a sexist remark, and the effect this might have had on the female members of the group.

As his practice teacher, consider each of the *Action techniques* categories in turn and make five sets of notes about what you could do to help him with this problem, using methods in each category.

Select the methods you think would have the best impact.

Notes for practice teachers

Chapters 13, 14 and 15 centred on the *content* of the practice learning. This and the following two chapters focus on the *methods* used to promote the student's learning.

The supervision session, or practice tutorial, is a focal point for the student's learning. It is surprising, therefore, that we know relatively little about what actually goes on during it. Only recently, with the requirement for direct observation of candidates for the Practice Teaching Award and for video presentations of practice tutorials (required by some programmes), has the veil begun to lift.

This chapter advocates the development of a wide range of teaching methods. These methods are not confined to the practice tutorial, but it is important to incorporate them into these sessions.

Traditional approaches to supervision

Different models of practice teaching were described in Chapter 1, and you plotted your own experience of practice teaching and learning (either as a student or as a practice teacher). Using this book in preparation for the Practice Teacher Award has provided you with direct experience of the structured learning approach.

We use the term *'practice tutorial'* as opposed to 'supervision session' as a means of distinguishing different models of teaching. Student supervision is too often modelled on practitioners' own experience of supervision in the agency, which is not appropriate for practice teaching.

Traditional approaches to supervision have come under increasing criticism. In particular, Gardiner (1989: 11) analyses the limitations of an approach where 'learning is equated with the emotional growth of the student and learning problems are the fault of the student's assumed emotional difficulties'. He describes the process of 'concept leakage' – from the practice of social casework into accounts of the supervisory relationship – and he details eight features of the classical model:

- '*student learning is synonymous with emotional growth*'
- 'the *focus is on individuals rather than on interactions between them*'
- '*problems are seen and described as pathologies* in the growth and development of individuals'
- 'there is *a hierarchical, traditional teacher–learner relationship* and a similar pattern is *replicated in the relative status of tutors and supervisors*'
- 'there is an emphasis on *the authority of the discipline* itself, and *what* is taught *rather than on how students learn*'
- '*the practice arena is seen as an illustration* of college-based teaching, and an *opportunity to apply previous instruction in practice*'
- '*students are assumed to be relatively homogenous* in style and stage of learning, so no account is taken of individual differences between teachers and learners'
- 'there are *no significant differences between teachers in HOW they teach.*' (Gardiner, 1989: 16; original emphases)

Action techniques

As far as it is possible to know, the traditional approach to supervision has relied on discussion as the dominant method of teaching. Over recent years, there has been a move towards using a greater range of teaching techniques. Catherine Sawdon (1985) has produced a taxonomy of techniques available to practice teachers (see page 129). This details the enormous variety of teaching methods, using five separate categories, plus a sixth section which considers the arrangements for the teaching. 'The term [action techniques] seeks to identify those resources which can be brought into the "action" to assist learning and to gather assessment evidence. These can be distinguished from "interaction" techniques' (Sawdon and Sawdon, 1988).

These action techniques are not mutually exclusive – in the course of any particular teaching theme it is possible that activities in all five categories will be included.

Example

Jenny asked Saj, her practice teacher, to include 'Self-Presentation' (one of the units of the practice curriculum) on the agenda for the next practice tutorial, following an incident she felt she had handled badly. Saj asked Jenny to write a critical incident analysis (Category 2: Written) in relation to the event in question, in preparation for the practice tutorial. At the beginning of the session they used the flip-chart (Category 4: Graphic) to brainstorm the main points which had come out of the critical incident analysis, and then discussed what Jenny had learned from the episode and how she would like to handle it next time (Category 3: Experiential). They agreed to re-play the incident via a role-play (Category 3: Experiential), which they wanted to video-tape, but the video was booked out so they audio-taped instead (Category 1: Hardware). After listening to the audio tape and discussing it, Saj and Jenny looked at the learning objectives in the 'Self-Presentation' unit of the practice curriculum (Category 5: Printed) to evaluate Jenny's progress. Saj gave Jenny a newspaper article (Category 5: Printed) which was relevant to the issues and which he thought she might like to read later.

A practice tutorial which uses a variety of teaching methods is likely to be more stimulating than one which relies on a single method of learning and discovery. The example above is illustrative of an active approach to teaching, combining the needs of the particular student, the practice teacher's tool-kit and the framework of the practice curriculum. There are times when the student is not so self-aware as Jenny, in which case Saj would take more of a lead in setting the agenda; however, you should try to maintain a balance between items initiated by you and those initiated by the student.

Organizing the practice tutorial

Preparation

It is important that you and the student contribute to an agenda before the session, so that you are both able to prepare adequately. There are very few teachers who meet their students without some preparation – think of a group of students going to class-based teaching where the teacher had no prepared material. The agency setting is not the same as the college, but lack of preparation is likely to lead to a heavy reliance on discussion, which in turn can lead to drift.

The agenda should contain some items which are related to the student's specific work with clients and community groups, etc. (a 'round-up') and others concerned with issues and themes. Moving between the specific and the general, and helping the student to make connections between the two, is part of your craft as a practice teacher. Students should know what specific preparations you would like them to make (bring certain case files up to date, read a particular article, complete a certain exercise, etc.).

A typical agenda will have items which fall into these categories:

- report of direct work with 'cases' and allocation of work (clients, residents, community groups, etc.)
- problem-solving (exploring particular concerns and exploring options for resolution)
- theme teaching (focus on a particular aspect of professional practice)
- review of progress (relating the student's work and learning to the programme curriculum and the Learning Agreement – see Chapter 5)
- planning future learning opportunities (keeping an eye on the pace of the work and progress with the curriculum)
- any special issues

The practice tutorial

The practice tutorial is only one forum for practice learning. Your direct work together (see Chapter 18) and informal chats over coffee, as well as all the other contacts with colleagues and clients, are opportunities for the student's learning. However, a practice tutorial of one to two hours at a regular time at least once a week gives the opportunity to put this learning into focus and for any specific teaching themes to be introduced.

The practice tutorial is a complex meeting, combining many elements related to your different functions as a practice teacher. These all require 'changes in gear', and failure to recognize the need for these changes can prevent the session from achieving the best results. Some elements are *formal and managerial* (e.g. those relating to the supervision of the quality of service to users); others are *didactic and information-giving* (e.g. explaining the relevance of agency policy to a particular piece of practice); others are *exploratory and reflective* (e.g. encouraging the student to think about different options in the work with a client), and yet others are *supportive and confidence-building* (e.g. giving encouragement about the student's work by helping to confront an emotional block).

Butler and Elliott (1985: 65–8) describe three functions of student supervision – management, helping and educative – and Ford and Jones (1987: 69–72) pinpoint four stages – descriptive, clarification, evaluative and implementation.

Our understanding of what happens in practice tutorials is too limited to know how these elements are understood by practice teachers and students, but you might find it useful to video a session (with the student's agreement, of course), name the different elements of the session, and analyse how you moved between the different functions described above.

After the practice tutorial

Both you and the student should decide how practice tutorials will be recorded. Students might want to make notes in their practice files, according to the different units in the practice curriculum; you, too, need to collect information in such a way as to help you compile the assessment report. If you are also collecting samples of your own practice teaching (for the Practice Teaching Award), it is useful to have a ring-binder divided into the relevant sections, so that you can compile your portfolio over time (see Chapter 22).

Taking five minutes at the end of each session to summarize the work of the session in terms of the content, the learning and any action which you and the student have agreed to undertake is a helpful reminder at the start of the next tutorial. This summary should be kept in the same place as the agenda sheet for the next session.

Arrangements for practice tutorials

The term 'supervision session' is often identified with one-to-one teaching. This opportunity for close tuition is very valuable and is likely to continue to be the preferred arrangement. However, there are many other arrangements which are available, and it is important that one-to-one teaching is chosen actively and not by default (see page 129; see also Payne and Scott, 1982).

There are many reasons why opportunities for learning in small groups should be considered, not least the different perspectives which other people bring to professional practice and the sense of support which students get from each other (Bogo and Vayda, 1987: 69–70). Consider bringing a number of practice teachers together as well as a number of students, because it is often instructive for students to see the perspectives of different practitioners, too. Much of the activity-based learning in Doel and Shardlow (1993) benefits from small group learning in which a number of practice teachers and students take part.

The main principle to guide your practice in the practice tutorial is active choice. If the arrangements for practice tutorials are always one-to-one, and they consist solely of discussion, it is an indicator that you are not considering alternatives and that your practice teaching has become habitual rather than responsive.

The choice of methods and arrangements is guided by at least three factors:

- the student's individual learning profile (and willingness to experiment)
- your repertoire of teaching methods (and willingness to expand this)
- the particular framework of the curriculum for the DipSW

Variety for variety's sake is to be avoided, but most people enjoy a change of style and pace, and it will make the practice tutorial more fun for you as well as for the student if you can vary both the menu and the venue.

The practice teaching portfolio

Your portfolio should show evidence that you are aware of various methods of practice teaching and that you are able to make discriminating use of these different methods – in other words, it is not just a case of pulling 'a method' out of your tool-kit, but considering carefully what particular purpose this particular method serves with this particular student (or students) on this particular occasion.

It is more useful to highlight a few specific examples of how you used certain methods (and to evaluate this) than to make broad generalizations with no detailed illustrations.

As usual, check the guidelines for preparing a portfolio issued by your practice teaching programme. In general, it is useful for a portfolio to contain an analysis of at least one practice tutorial, and you may want to link this to any requirements for a video account – see Chapters 18 and 22.

Example 16

Janet described how she structured a practice tutorial around the theme of 'cultural competence'. She had two students, Maia and Roger, on placement in her unit, and they had agreed to have some sessions together with a colleague, Sandra, and her student, Dale.

Janet opened the session with a video taken from a TV soap as an example of 'cultural incompetence'. This triggered a lot of discussion, and, together, the group began to arrive at some statements of what they thought 'cultural

continued

---

competence' meant. Maia wrote these on a flip-chart. Janet then gave out pho-tocopies of 'You Are What You Eat' (Doel and Shardlow, 1993: 159) to trigger discussion about personal biography and valuing difference. This helped to move the group's thinking from ideas and concepts towards the personal, so they could experience differences and check personal assumptions.

Finally, Janet asked the students to introduce some examples from their recent work to illustrate what they had learned about cultural competence in this session. Each student and each practice teacher made a single statement of something they would do differently as a result of this practice tutorial.

Janet asked everybody for a brief written evaluation of the session and included this (anonymized) in her portfolio, and towards the end of the place-ment she asked Maia and Roger to reflect back on the session to see how useful it had turned out to be. Janet felt positive about the practice tutorial, but she thought it took the group a while to get to grips with the concept of 'cultural competence', and that next time she would make some brief reading available before the session. She described how Maia in particular made use of the concept of 'cultural competence' during other tutorial sessions. (See also the example of Saj and Jenny on page 131.)

17 Designing learning activities

About Activity 17   Jackdaw

The practice teacher's difficulty lies not in the search for teaching materials, but in the decision about which ones to select. The message in *Jackdaw* is that it is not necessary to spend hours of creative energy designing new activities – beg and borrow existing materials and adapt them to your own needs. *Jackdaw* takes a specific area of practice learning (skills of recording) and suggests you think widely in your collection of materials.

Purpose

This chapter highlights the use of structured activities to help the student's learning in preparation for direct work with clients. It offers a four-stage process to design and use teaching activities, and explores the value of simulated activities.

Method

- Take some time to digest the learning objectives for the example area (unit) of practice learning; what do the objectives mean in your setting, and are there any key points you want to highlight for the student?
- Open a file or folder. Over the next week or so keep this unit in the back of your mind, and collect materials which might help to teach it. Treat this as a 'quick-think' – in other words, don't spend time evaluating whether each item will be useful, just stick it in the folder as it crosses your path.
- After a week, sort through the materials you have collected. Using the guidelines on pages 139–40, design an activity to use with a student.
- Give the activity a test-run.

Variations

You may prefer to use the *Jackdaw* method with an alternative area of learning. In fact, if you coordinate your work with other practice teachers to develop activities for different units of learning, together you could cover the full curriculum.

Activity 17   Jackdaw

This is an example of a unit of practice learning, another piece of the 'jigsaw' described in Chapter 14. It is taken from a Placement One Module 3, 'Working in the Agency' (South Yorkshire, 1993).

Consider the learning objectives for this area of practice. In part, they cluster around the student's ability to record within the agency's requirements; in part, they are concerned with how the student involves the agency's clients in recording the work.

Example unit: Skills in recording

Description

This unit teaches the use of the social work record to satisfy agency requirements and to share with the service user.

Learning objectives

The student should demonstrate an ability to:

1   Understand the purposes and limits of agency and unit records.
2   Write clear, concise records to meet these purposes.
3   Differentiate facts from opinions in records and understand the implications of stereotyping and labelling in recording.
4   Share the records with the service user as part of the work, taking into account power relationships around race, gender, sexuality, HIV status, etc.
5   Understand the laws in relation to the use of written information.
6   Begin to analyse not only what records contain, but equally what information is omitted. This is especially important in relation to developing anti-oppressive practice and service provision.

Note: You can substitute a unit or area of practice learning from your local Diploma in Social Work programme for this suggested unit.

Over the next week, collect materials as you come across them which you could use to help the student's learning in this area – examples from case records or the day book, newspaper items, agency policy documents, articles, illustrations from fiction, etc. At the end of the week, review your materials and use some of them to design an activity which teaches skills in recording (there is guidance on pages 139–40).

Cooperate with another 'jackdaw' and you will have twice as much material.

Notes for practice teachers

The value of activity-based learning is not confined to people who are Activists (see Chapter 11). By 'activity', we mean a coherent set of actions whose purpose is to promote the student's learning, and this could include a quiet period of reflective reading. Indeed, there are plenty of different ways in which the activity can be presented – the medium or method. Moreover, an activity can be ready-made (such as a written trigger exercise) or spontaneous (like a 'quick-think'). It can be 'live', in direct contact with users of the agency's services, or 'simulated' – designed to reproduce or parallel practice issues in some way. This chapter provides some guidelines for designing and using activities in practice teaching.

Four stages in the design and use of an activity

1   The rationale

It is important that the student shares your understanding of the significance of the area of practice learning which the activity is designed to promote. If it is very broadly relevant, give specific examples to anchor it. Motivation will increase if the student understands the benefits of developing skills or knowledge in this area and the consequences of not doing so.

Questions to consider:

- Who identified this area of practice – you or the student?
- Is it an area where the student feels confident, or uncertain?
- How does it fit with the student's needs at this time?

When students can see a direct relationship between the activity and their own learning needs, they are likely to commit themselves fully.

2   The activity

Once the relevance of the particular area of practice has been established, it is important to think about how to shape this into an *opportunity for learning*.

There are many different kinds of activity, but let's break these into two main groups – live activities and simulated activities.

Live activities are those which involve learning from direct practice, with individuals, families and groups. The practice teacher might be present at the learning opportunity in a relatively active way, such as live supervision in the same room (Evans, 1987), or in a more passive way, such as 'sitting next to Nellie', as an industrial apprentice watches an experienced worker operate a machine. Live activities are discussed in more detail in Chapter 18.

Simulated activities are those which involve learning from indirect practice – for example, a written exercise, a video, a role-play, a photograph, etc. may be used to trigger issues or rehearse practice dilemmas. We are not confining the term to *simulations* (faithful reproductions of live practice), but include any activity designed to promote the student's learning outside live practice.

When devising an activity, practice teachers need to ask themselves what *medium* or *combination of media* they want to use (discussion, action, written, video, etc.), and what *arrangements*. It is best not to agonize about this, but make sure over the length of the placement that the student is exposed to a range of media and arrangements (see Chapter 16).

3   The learning points

Whatever is learned from an activity needs to be named, so that you and the student are aware of the learning that has taken place. Naming and recording the learning which has taken place helps to make it active rather than passive.

Passive learning occurs implicitly – for example, the cultural significance of many activities is generally learned passively. Our learning may be excellent, in terms of the ability to reproduce our own culture's behaviours, but the implicit nature of the learning limits the possibility of change or challenge. Exposure to other cultural behaviours may be interpreted as others' *lack* of learning rather than others' *different* learning.

Active learning is overt and practised, where the process of learning is explicit. Social learning can be made conscious, even though it is usually implicit. Active learning is essential to anti-oppressive practice because it is an empowering rather than a mystifying experience for the learner, who is likely to feel more in control of the process. It helps the learner to understand diversity and difference; with understanding comes the possibility of valuing.

The student's portfolio or placement file is a good place to keep track of these learning points and to register the student's development as a practitioner.

4   The practice

'You can talk it, but can you walk it?' – so reads the slogan on one US T-shirt. It is important to chart how the learning which has taken place as a result of the activity gets transferred by students into their live practice. How is the learning being integrated into practice? In other words, the student should show an ability to:

- understand the relevance of the learning to practice
- put the learning into practice
- make links with other aspects of their practice

It takes time to find out whether this fourth stage has been completed successfully.

The value of simulated activities

Taking risks

Simulated activities provide a safety net for practice. They take place without direct impact on users of the service, so it is possible to lessen the consequences of taking risks (including the emotional risks of exposing feelings and personal values). If needs be, the practice teacher can suspend 'quality control' temporarily while the student tests the limits. Using a simple metaphor: you find the boundaries of an unknown, unlit room by feeling round the outer walls, not by taking cautious steps around the centre. The student needs to get a feel for these outer walls by pressing at them, and this is possible if the consequences do not put real people at risk.

Accelerated learning

Judged by the telephone directory of competencies expected of students by some social work training programmes, you might expect the average placement to last a year. However, most placements are relatively short, and the time must be used to maximum effect. The student might strike it lucky sitting around in the day room, or hanging about for duty calls, but it is a high-risk strategy to hope that something will turn up. It is also an example of passive learning, where, even if something does happen, the student may be ill-prepared to learn from it, or could learn poor rather than good practice.

   The value of simulated activities is their potential to accelerate the student's learning, to provide breakthroughs which live activities might not achieve. Doel (1988: 51–2) describes an example of accelerated learning through simulated practice, where a ten-minute activity to prioritize an 'in-tray' of pressing situations helped a student learn about his own criteria for taking action, in a way that was unlikely to have happened through a 'real' experience.

   Simulated activities enable you and the student to introduce a sense of *sequence* into the learning. This is not to suggest that we should see the student's learning as linear or chronological, but as *incremental*. In other words, the student may need to develop skills in one area before embarking on another, and this progress will differ from student to student. Live activities can produce opportunities for learning which the student is not 'ready' for; sometimes this is successful, oftentimes it is not. Simulated activities can be more closely tailored to the individual student's pace and stage of learning.

Fun

Finally, simulated activities are fun. At the risk of stating the obvious, learning is most likely to take place when all the participants are enjoying themselves. Activities which look at social work from a different angle, through a different doorway, turn it upside down and put it into reverse, can provide a welcome *digestif* to a diet of case files and personal care plans. Make good use of the fact that your work as a practice teacher is about developing a reflective practitioner, not instructing a procedural technician. This gives you enormous scope for creativity.

Advantages and disadvantages of live and simulated activities

Advantages (Live)	*Advantages (Simulated)*
● 'nothing like real life' ● spontaneous ● new ● tests the student in unprepared circumstances ● more natural ● immediacy value ● shows what student is like on an 'off day'; a better test	● tests out ideas, rehearse, reflect ● safe environment, less risky ● deals with problem dilemmas at the student's own pace ● phases activities appropriately ● better preparation; more focused ● practice teacher can be more organized ● provides opportunities that may not otherwise arise
Disadvantages (Live)	*Disadvantages (Simulated)*
● threatening to be 'watched' ● student can feel a 'spare part' ● sense of having to perform ● intrusive to clients; can be de-skilling ● feeling of needing to be perfect ● not phased; can learn poor practice ● 'real' practice might be at wrong level for the student	● loses the spark of live activities ● might still have difficulties *doing* it – 'You can talk it, but can you walk it?' ● unreal ● might miss some of the real issues ● no thinking on your feet ● hard to build in spontaneity

These items were the results of a 'quick-think' with practice teachers to identify the advantages and disadvantages of live and simulated learning.

The practice teaching portfolio

It is not necessary to produce lots of original, creative activities for your portfolio – it is difficult for a busy practitioner to find the time to design brand-new activities. However, you should include evidence of your ability to find and use existing activities, and to adapt them to your own setting and the needs of an individual student. If you have evidence of instances when the student's learning has *accelerated*, all the better.

Put the emphasis on *how* you used the activity, rather than a lengthy description of the activity itself.

Example 17

Maureen and Paul are practice teachers in the same unit, and they often do co-teaching. They have developed some activities together and some separately. When Maureen put her portfolio together, she included a brief list of some of the activities which she and Paul have used together. The collaboration with Paul is important to Maureen, but she also understood that the Practice Teaching Award is an individual award, so she described her own part in developing activities.

Maureen looked specifically at an exercise which she has adapted from *Learning Good Practice in Community Care* (CCETSW/OLF, 1993). She explained what the original activity was, how and why she adapted it, and evaluated how useful it was for the student's learning. She included a brief piece from Paul, who has also used Maureen's adaptation.

18 Direct observation and the use of video

About Activity 18   Triggers

Triggers is a way of using video to help the student's practice learning. The video might be commercially produced for social work, or just taken from a soap opera like *East Enders*. The activity goes on to describe a process which uses live video of your work with the student.

Purpose

Within the term 'direct observation' we include *live teaching* methods, the use of live video recording, and observing students' practice for assessment purposes. Direct observation is seen as *a process* when describing teaching and learning functions, and *an event* when describing assessment functions. The model of direct observation presented on pages 147–8 is a bridge between the teaching and supervisory functions in practice teaching.

This chapter also offers a series of steps for the video-shy.

Method

- Follow the steps outlined in the *Triggers* activity on page 146.
- For a detailed guide to *live teaching*, see Evans (1987).

Variations

By getting together with other practice teachers, it is possible to build a video library of useful scenes to illustrate skills and practices relevant to social work. Once the trigger questions have been written, they are likely to need only the occasional fine-tuning, in response to your experience of using them.

A *Triggers*-style activity is one you might consider for a project for the practice teaching portfolio.

Activity 18   Triggers

Using pre-recorded video for teaching purposes

Select a brief piece of pre-recorded video.

The video should illustrate an aspect of social work practice, directly or indirectly. This might be taken from a pre-recorded video made specifically for social work – for example, *Basic Skills for Practice Teachers* (Shardlow, 1988) or *Placement Triggers* (Shardlow and Doel, 1988). However, it need not be a social work video. For instance, you might find a scene from a soap opera where one of the characters challenges somebody else's beliefs – an illustration of a skill useful for social workers, but not exclusive to them.

Whatever video you use, make sure that it is relevant to the area of practice you are highlighting, and that the video excerpt is brief (less than five minutes).

Rather than ask the general question 'What did you think of that?', it is better to focus on two or three particular points which you think the scene raises, and to prompt the student to think of alternatives at specific points during the video – for example: 'When Margaret said "You surely can't think that that is the best way to stop him from doing that?", what did you think was the effect on Sylvie, and what would you have said at that point?'

You should review the video carefully before the practice teaching session to decide where you are going to stop the tape and what questions you are going to ask as a trigger to discussion of good practice. It is best to have these trigger questions written down, with a copy for the student.

Using live video for teaching purposes

When you and the student have become familiar with the use of pre-recorded video as a trigger to guide good practice, you should progress to live video. This might be a video of yourselves in role-play, or a video of work with a user or users of the agency (with their express permission, and proper safeguards about confidentiality and the use to which the video will be put).

Be clear about the purposes of the video – for example:

- to help you to develop your practice teaching skills
- as evidence of your practice teaching skills for your portfolio
- to help the student to develop practice skills
- as evidence of the student's practice skills
- to help a client to develop his or her social skills

Each of these purposes is equally valid, but it is important to agree the purpose beforehand so that you can be clear about your focus afterwards.

Notes for practice teachers

A model for direct observation

CCETSW require a student's practice 'to be directly and systematically observed by a practice teacher' (CCETSW, 1991b: 25). The limitations of a system where practitioners can be set loose on the public without their practice being seen have been described elsewhere, in analogy (Doel, 1987a) and parody (Shardlow, 1989a).

In some settings such as day care and group care, regular observation of the student's direct work with people is inevitable because it is an established feature of the work. In other settings, largely field work, there is little tradition of joint work or directly supervised work, so these kinds of opportunity have to be created. On the face of it, settings where direct observation is commonplace seem to have the advantage, but this is not necessarily the case. It can sometimes be more difficult to plan *systematic* observation where observation is routine and not formalized, than in circumstances where a plan has to be created. Whatever the setting, it is important to have a plan for direct observation, because the plan helps to clarify the purpose.

Planning

The student should know prior to the placement that direct observation will be a feature of the practice learning and assessment. The principal reasons for direct observation should be discussed with the student – the educational purposes, which enable you to give much better-quality feedback about the student's practice than student-report can achieve, and the supervisory purposes, which are essential for you to make judgements about the student's abilities and the quality of the work which the student's future clients can expect. A suggested process for direct observation should be sketched and agreed (see page 148).

Process

The first step is for you and the student to be honest about your response to direct observation. Some students welcome the opportunity for direct feedback about their work, others suffer from performance anxiety. It is important not to make any assumptions about the student's likely response, even though the tendency is to assume that they will be nervous. In their work on *The Practice Portfolio*, Doel and Shardlow (1989) were surprised to find that the students expected and desired more direct observation than they received.

Trust is an important aspect of direct observation, and one way of establishing trust is to invite the student to observe your own practice from the beginning of the placement. This helps students to get a feel for the work, to watch your approach and methods, and to understand that you are not going to ask them to do anything that you are not prepared to do yourself. It is good for the student to see you evaluating your own practice and for you to invite the student to take part in this appraisal. While not denying the power of your role as practice teacher, this kind of exposure helps to lessen the distance between you and the student.

It is right for you to take the lead in these first contacts, but the student should expect to take a more active role as confidence grows. The experience should feel increasingly like one of joint working, until the student feels ready to take the lead, with your own contribution tailing off.

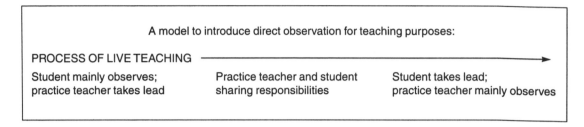

A model to introduce direct observation for teaching purposes:

PROCESS OF LIVE TEACHING

| Student mainly observes; practice teacher takes lead | Practice teacher and student sharing responsibilities | Student takes lead; practice teacher mainly observes |

Integrating the educational and supervisory roles

This model helps to balance the educational and supervisory purposes of direct observation. It carefully builds trust and familiarity, rather than the nervous anticipation of some future visitation. In settings where joint work is a part of the routine, it is still useful to plan the student's progress along this continuum. (See Evans, 1987, for an interesting account of the use of direct observation as a method of teaching – 'live teaching in the same room'.)

In the early stage of the direct observation model above, the practice teacher provides a role model: 'This is one way of doing it', rather than 'This is *the* way to do it.' As students gain in confidence, you would expect them to take more of a lead, with coaching and preparation before the direct encounter.

Direct observation for teaching and learning purposes can be seen as a *process* rather than an event. In contrast, direct observation for assessment purposes should be planned as an *event*. If you have been using direct observation as a teaching method, the student should be reasonably comfortable with your presence, because it will be familiar; this takes part of the anxiety out of the assessment event. Indeed, your presence could be a reassurance rather than a threat.

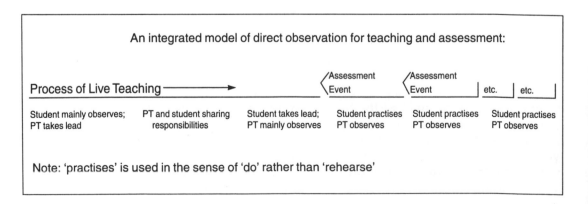

An integrated model of direct observation for teaching and assessment:

Process of Live Teaching

Assessment Event   Assessment Event   etc.   etc.

| Student mainly observes; PT takes lead | PT and student sharing responsibilities | Student takes lead; PT mainly observes | Student practises PT observes | Student practises PT observes | Student practises PT observes |

Note: 'practises' is used in the sense of 'do' rather than 'rehearse'

Assessment events should occur when students feel adequately prepared to have their learning tested (within the limits of the placement, of course). Your joint work with the student will have helped you to make informal assessments of the student's capabilities, and these evaluations should have formed the basis for your feedback to the student. However, these evaluations differ from formal assessment events, which focus on specific units of learning. Further guidance for planning assessment events is given in Chapter 20.

The process of live teaching need not stop with the onset of assessment events. Live teaching will continue around different themes, preparing for later assessment events which test the student's learning in the new area.

Making use of live activities when you are absent

How do you help the student learn from live activities when you are absent – for example, direct work with users of the service and direct contacts with colleagues in meetings when you are not present to guide or monitor? Students' learning will be enhanced and accelerated if they know what to look for (remember the notion of *active learning* described on page 140. This means confronting what Senge (1990: 23–4) calls 'the delusion of learning from experience'. The fact is that the student might or might not learn from experience, and the learning might be good or poor – there is nothing inherent in experience which makes it beneficial as a means of learning.

If you cannot guide practice by being present with the student, think about ways of guiding practice by proxy – for example, developing a written schedule with pointers to help the student focus the learning from the live activity. If your simulated activities have been well timed, these will also help to guide the student's practice (Chapter 17). Students should become increasingly able to monitor and guide their own practice, as a self-reflective learner and practitioner. When there is evidence that this is happening, students can assume much greater responsibility for their own learning, but it is a mistake to assume that the student knows how to do this from the start. Indeed, Senge (1990: 25) claims that the contrary is likely in most agencies, with practitioners learning to develop *skilled incompetence*.

Using video

There are many different uses of video in practice teaching (Shardlow, 1989b). In this chapter, we focus on how you can use it to video your own practice teaching.

Many people find using video a trial, and you may be one of them. Both in terms of using the machinery of video and of looking at and hearing the end result, you might prefer a visit to the dentist! Even worse for a videophobe is contact with a videophile, whose greatest joy is to perform in front of the lens.

The videophobe quite rightly asks 'Why bother?' Here are four good reasons:

- The single most compelling reason for making a video of your practice teaching is *feedback*. Nothing can replicate the unvarnished feedback of video.
- Once you have acquired video skills, you can transfer these to students so they

are able to make videos of their own practice to gain direct feedback about their own work. (Some students will have more video experience than you, and they can teach you the technicalities.)

- You may be required to submit a video as part of your practice portfolio (depending on the programme), and it makes sense to make a quality video for this purpose.
- The more practice you have with the video, the more it will become a routine method of obtaining regular feedback about your practice teaching.

Chapter 22 looks at preparing a video and a written evaluation of the video for your portfolio.

Four stages to get the best from video

You wouldn't take a car on the road before you learned to drive; similarly, you shouldn't include video equipment in your practice teaching before you know how to use it properly.

1   Start with a self-assessment

Where are you on this continuum?:

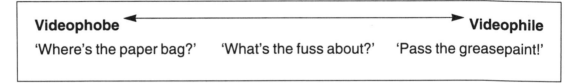

Wherever you place yourself, make a list of the things which most concern or attract you to video, and share these with somebody else. This is one way of making your fears and joys public. It is especially important for the videophobe to confront what the fear is. The experienced videophile can skip the next two stages.

2   Locate your equipment and know how it works

Find out what equipment your agency has available (you will probably be surprised at what is lurking in remote cupboards at the farthest reaches). Since most equipment manuals seem to be written for people who live on Planet Zog, it is important to get a hands-on demonstration of how the equipment works if you are new to it (record and play-back). Colour-coding helps to cue which lead goes to which terminal.

3   Combat the cosmetic effect

Become familiar with your video image in relatively friendly surroundings. The best way of doing this is to take the equipment home and play with it. Ask friends or family to video you informally around the house, so that when you play it back you get used to how you look; video is very different from still photographs, and your own gestures and movements will seem new to you. Get used to these now, before bringing the video into your work life.

4   *Focus on quality*

The quality of the content is irrelevant if the quality of presentation is so poor that it cannot be heard or people's faces cannot be seen (so non-verbal responses are lost). In other words: test the recording before you begin to video. Avoid videoing against the light, so make sure that windows are behind the camera where possible, and check that the microphone can pick up what is being said, and so on. It may not be Hollywood, but there is no point in putting yourself and your student through a recording session if it is not possible to see or hear the result. Remember, too, that it is not necessary to have somebody behind the camera; you can take a static shot, positioning the camera so that you are both on screen. Often, the most successful angle is one where you, the student and the camera are set at equal angles to each other.

Use the *Triggers* activity (page 146) to help you make the best use of your video.

The practice teaching portfolio

Direct and systematic observation of a student's practice is a requirement for the Diploma in Social Work, so you will need to demonstrate in your portfolio how you have put this requirement into practice.

The use of video is one teaching method available to you as an aid to the student's practice learning. However, it is not a requirement. If you have used video in your work with the student, briefly evaluate how this worked.

Example 18

Shula evaluated how she used the model to introduce direct observation for teaching purposes with her student, Simone. She highlighted what had worked best about this method, and pinpointed a couple of aspects which did not work so well, and how she thought she would do this differently with her next student.

Shula familiarized herself with the video, learning the technicalities from Simone, who had used video extensively on her previous placement. In the end, Shula developed a role-play with Simone which she video-taped. She wrote a series of trigger questions with some 'Notes for the Practice Teacher' attached to each trigger question, so that the video could be used by other practice teachers and students (Simone gave her permission for this). Shula included this piece of work in her portfolio as the project.

Module 7

Examination of Ability

19 The assessment climate

About Activity 19   'L' plates

In this chapter we link the twin themes of *learning* and *assessment*. The tension between these themes should be acknowledged openly. This chapter helps you to integrate learning and assessment, in terms of looking at the importance of the learning environment as providing a climate for a fair assessment.

Purpose

'L' plates helps you to 'tune in' to the kinds of feelings which the student may have about assessment. The learning climate which we explored in Chapter 11 is an important backdrop for the assessment of students, who should be aware of the 'rules of the game' and how these will govern the assessment of their practice ability. Some of these rules are set by the Diploma in Social Work programme, and some are dependent on your style and approach.

Method

Use the *'L' plates* activity to trigger your thoughts about the impact of assessment:

- Jot down the memory of your thoughts and feelings before, during and after your driving test (if you have not taken a driving test, use another similar episode, such as a piano examination).
- Take each of the questions in the leg of the 'L' and make some comparisons between assessment outside and inside the social work context.
- Finally, consider the different words used for assessing functions, found in the foot of the 'L'. How do these differ in their meanings, and what are their different implications?

Variations

This is a useful activity to carry out with a small group of practice teachers (and with a student group), so that you can elicit a variety of opinions and responses to assessment.

Activity 19   'L' plates

The driving test is a common experience of being tested.

Jot down the memory of your thoughts and feelings before, during and after the driving test. How do these memories help you to think about the assessment climate for the social work student?

Take each of the following issues in turn. In what ways are the assessment processes in social work and driving similar and dissimilar? Any other issues you would add?

- clear criteria for competence
- cues for when assessment is taking place
- clear criteria for failure
- an established appeals procedure
- evidence provided by direct observation
- evidence provided by written reports
- assessment is over a period of time
- assessment is a single event
- assessment of a narrow range of skills
- assessment covers values and beliefs
- result of assessment has a major impact
- decision made by one person or a group
- etc.

How would you define the following?

An adjudication is ....

An appraisal is ....

An assessment is ....

An evaluation is ....

An examination is ....

A judgement is ....

A review is ....

A test is ....

Which one most closely approximates to the process which decides whether a student social worker will be awarded the Diploma in Social Work?

Notes for practice teachers

During the last few years, there has been a broad move towards competency-based assessment in a wide range of vocational activities. In part, this reflects a 'tougher' outlook towards professional and other workers, to make them more effective, efficient and accountable; in part, it is a reaction to the power and paternalism of the professions and the welfare bureaucracies. Social work does not stand apart from other vocations, such as nursing and teaching, which are also under review by the National Council for Vocational Qualifications (NCVQ, but SCOTVEC in Scotland). For good or ill, there are increasing demands that we make the social work task explicit and, as a practice teacher, you have a particular responsibility to articulate this task.

It is important for you to be honest to yourself about your initial response to the approach to assessment detailed in these three chapters (19, 20 and 21). 'Performance', 'competence' and 'curriculum' have become highly politicized words, and your learning in these areas could easily be blocked by negative associations (see Chapter 12). Whatever your response to the political direction of these changes, it will become apparent that there are a number of advantages and disadvantages to these approaches to assessment, and that you have considerable power as an individual practice teacher to create a fair (or unfair) assessment climate for the student.

CCETSW's documents about the Diploma in Social Work reflect current trends, emphasizing assessment in a way that is likely to encourage programmes to review their existing assessment systems (Evans, 1992: 9). In Chapter 20 you will find principles to guide the assessment of an *individual* student's practice. Below are four principles to develop a *system* for assessment (Doel and Shardlow, 1989: 8).

A system for assessment: Four principles

Accuracy

Whatever system of assessment is devised, it should be reliable and valid, to allow an accurate reflection of the student's abilities. For example, consider how the medium can influence this accuracy: does the practice teacher's report reflect the author's ability to write a report rather than the student's competence in social work; does a video tape demonstrate the filmer's abilities to use the equipment; does a case history show the writer's literary skills; does a client feedback form illustrate the degree of satisfaction with the outcome of the work, to the exclusion of the process? These are all commonly-held views. What kind of system of assessment reflects the student's competence *accurately*?

Fairness

Any system which examines the practice of a person training for professional work must be seen to be fair and just. Is there a proper balance between the examiner's desire for the rigorous scrutiny of practice, the students' wishes to present good examples of their work, and the interests and protection of users in the kind of service which they receive or would like to receive?

The system should deal with the individual student justly and be seen to be fair across the system, from student to student. This means positive action where certain assessment methods are known to disadvantage some groups of students.

Efficiency

Assessment methods and procedures need to make the best use of time. A system might be very accurate and fair, but unacceptable if it consumes a large proportion of the student's learning time, or the assessor's examination time. We have few accurate measurements of the amount of time which assessment takes (or the balance between the time taken by teacher and learner). Doel and Shardlow (1989) advocated the use of a practice portfolio for students in order to give the larger part of the responsibility for presenting evidence to the student. Participants in that project gave mixed responses about the time which the portfolio method took; interestingly, those who completed the most practice assignments were the most positive about the time taken.

Congruence

Finally, what effect do different methods of assessment have on the student's learning? Do some methods help to enhance learning more than others? The question at issue is the possibility of congruence, or 'a fit', between the methods used to aid the student's learning, the student's actual practice and the examination of that practice. For example, perhaps an unseen written examination produces improvements in the short-term learning of facts, but a less enduring grasp of underlying principles? What system of examination, or particular methods of assessment, will enhance the student's learning?

Some responses to these issues are provided in this and the following two chapters.

Power and an anti-discriminatory framework for assessment

The best way to create a good climate for assessment is for you and the student to discuss the issues and the choices. It is crucial for there to be a common understanding of the general system of examination and the specific methods of assessment. You each need to be aware of who will be responsible for what, and how you will sample the student's work (see Chapter 20). A discussion of assessment will also address the issue of power directly; this does not lessen your powers and responsibilities as a practice teacher, but it does take them out of the realm of fantasy and into a form which makes them concrete.

The importance of a shared understanding of the rules of assessment is underlined by Gardiner (1989: 63), reporting on research conducted in Sweden: 'those students who are able to accurately identify the nature of the assessment task (*cue-seekers*) may be better able than other students to adjust their learning strategies to fit course assessment requirements'. In other words: the cue that the driving examiner's tap on the dashboard is the signal for you to carry out an emergency stop is a considerable help to your learning strategies before the test. Whether cue-seeking is 'a good thing' or not, it is only fair that all students should have knowledge of the nature of the assessment task.

The frequent use of the word 'assessment' in social work is a source of confusion, and it can prevent proper cue-taking. Gardiner (1989: 52–3) describes a tape of a practice teacher and a student in a supervision session where 'it is not immediately clear that the student realizes that the supervisor [practice teacher] is talking about assessing *him* rather than *his* [the student's] assessment of the family in the case they are discussing'.

Evans (1992: 19) describes four ways to empower student participation in assessment:

- Students are thoroughly informed about the assessment process and are given cues by way of criteria and models of good-enough practice.
- Students are provided with a range and choice of assessment methods.
- Students are given the right of reply to all assessment judgements.
- Students are able to organize their response to assessment in groups.

Peer group support can be particularly important to counter discriminatory treatment of a student (Ahmed et al., 1988). Peer support is also useful for you as a practice teacher, to increase your confidence in making assessment judgements (see Chapter 21).

Your choice of assessment methods is an important aspect of creating a fair climate for the student. There will be some methods which you use with every student (for example, direct observation), but – as Sawdon and Sawdon (1988: 77) point out – it is possible to tailor the range of assessment methods to the individual learning styles of each student, and to involve the student in those choices.

The impact of assessment on learning

Some negative aspects

It is not uncommon to experience assessment as a pressure which can block learning and inhibit performance, so that the assessed person does not feel as if they have given their best. It is impossible to eliminate this pressure, but you can reduce the anxiety by being clear about the purposes and the groundrules for assessment. Working under pressure is, in itself, an inescapable aspect of social work and it is important to learn skills to cope with this pressure. Some of the sting can be taken out of assessment if students familiarize themselves with the assessment process by rehearsing it (see Chapter 20).

The knowledge that work is being assessed can lead to an unwillingness to take risks, which can impoverish the opportunities for learning. Sampling students' work for assessment in a planned way can free them to take risks in other unassessed areas of their work – for example, knowing that their responses are not going to be assessed can free a student to discuss an activity like 'Boundaries' honestly and openly (in Doel and Shardlow, 1993: 23–4).

Assessment can be a time-consuming activity which distracts from the focus on learning. Integrating assessment with practice, so that activities for assessment are not additional to the work itself, is one way of limiting the impact of assessment on the time available for learning.

Some positive aspects

There is an understandable tendency to dwell on the inhibiting aspects of assessment. Yet the knowledge that work is going to be assessed can be a tremendous motivator, too.

A positive reframing of assessment is to view it as *feedback with consequences*. Many of the aspects of giving and receiving feedback discussed in Chapter 10 apply to assessment, with the added difference that *Assessment = Feedback + Power*. The consequences of the feedback are great when they are backed by the power of assessment.

Examinations can be affirming experiences. For example, it is possible to study the piano for your own personal enjoyment, without any feedback about your performance. However, the public scrutiny of an examination provides an independent affirmation of the quality of your playing (Grade 5, etc.), which can build your confidence. This knowledge gives students confidence to practise, too. Whether the feedback is affirming or challenging, positive or negative, the student's response is a good indicator of their future potential. A student who is serious about becoming a professional will take feedback that their practice is lacking as an opportunity for further learning.

The ultimate purpose of assessment is very positive: a safeguard to social work clients and a guarantee of professional standards. It is right to do all you can to make the climate for assessment a positive one, and the assessment itself is justified because of the need for these safeguards.

The practice teaching portfolio

Your portfolio should demonstrate an understanding of the conflict between assessment and learning and how you have attempted to provide a positive context in which the student's practice can be assessed.

Make sure you point to difficulties as well as successes in achieving a fair climate for the assessment.

Example 19

In the example in Chapter 18 (page 151), Shula demonstrated the way she had used direct observation in her work with Simone, using the approach described on page 148. In Chapter 20 (page 173), she demonstrates how she adapted the *Yardsticks* approach to one particular aspect of Simone's practice competence, and subsequently, how Simone used this model to assess a piece of her own work.

For the area of practice teaching covered in this chapter, Shula briefly described how she interpreted what 'creating a climate for assessment' meant in her own setting, and in the context of herself as a black woman assessing the competence of Simone, a white woman. She compiled a short questionnaire, which she asked Simone to complete at the end of the placement (after the assessment document had been sent), explaining that she would like to include the questionnaire in her portfolio. Shula wrote a brief commentary to Simone's reponses.

These are the questions she asked:

The assessment climate for S.L.'s placement

- What were *your feelings* at the beginning of the placement about being assessed?
- What do you think was *fair* and what *unfair* about the way your work was assessed?
- What *other methods* would you have liked me to use to assess your work?
- Are there any aspects where you think my assessment was too *positive*?
- Are there any aspects where you think my assessment was too *negative*?
- Give me some *advice* for when I next have a student – for example, how could I improve the climate for assessment?

20 Criteria for competence

About Activity 20   Yardsticks

Yardsticks provides a model to help you to develop criteria for competence in specific areas of practice and in collaboration with the student. This provides both a model of assessment and a means by which students can learn how to assess their own practice. To this extent it is a method of assessment which is 'congruent' with the student's learning needs.

Purpose

The previous chapter discussed the climate for assessment, the integration of learning and assessment, and how the two influence each other. This chapter focuses on the separation of learning and assessment, exploring the distinction between learning *processes* and assessment *events*.

Method

- For this exercise, you can work either in a pair with your student or in a small group of practice teachers and/or students.
- Spend about twenty minutes to develop criteria, then observe a sample of relevant practice (via a segment of video tape or a role-play).
- Use the agreed criteria to assess the practice as demonstrated on the video.

Variations

Yardsticks has been used as a training exercise with larger groups of practice teachers. In this case, the large group splits into three or four smaller groups, and each small group uses the criteria of one of the other groups, rather than their own. This sharpens the need for clarity when developing criteria.

The particular example on pages 165–7 uses a trigger from a video tape produced by the Joint Unit for Social Services Research at Sheffield University (Marsh and Bayley, 1984). Any other similar five- to ten-minute video tape of social work practice can be used (or you can make your own) to illustrate other areas of practice.

Alternatively, you can use a role-play as an example of practice.

The *Yardsticks* model can be used with any identified piece of social work practice, and once you have rehearsed it as an exercise, you should try using it directly with the student's own practice. You should always develop criteria together with the student.

Important note: please complete each activity before *reading the next one.*

Activity 20   Yardsticks (1)

Included in your student's learning objectives for the placement is:

● to develop helping skills with people in distress, and especially the skill of expressing empathy

As the practice teacher, you have said that you will provide an opportunity for this during the placement.

Developing criteria

You are going to develop criteria to assess the student's work in this area.

You can do this together with the student, or in a small group of practice teachers and/or students. It has been agreed that the student's practice will be assessed using only the agreed criteria.

● What are the criteria of good practice for helping people in distress and expressing empathy?

You may find it helpful to brainstorm a list of factors and then prioritize them into four or five main points. Make your final list as *specific* as possible, so that it could be understood by other practice teachers who have not been involved in your discussions.

Write down your criteria as clearly as possible (use a sheet of flip-chart paper if you are doing this as a large group exercise).

Activity 20   Yardsticks (2)

Sampling practice

The criteria which have been developed now need to be used with a sample of practice.

For the purposes of a training exercise, a short piece of video is the most effective way of doing this (or video-taping a short role-play, and playing this back). For example, there is a ten-minute scene of practice which illustrates a student expressing empathy with a distressed client in the video *Social Skills and Social Work* (Marsh and Bayley, 1984, fifth scene).

If you are using another group's criteria rather than your own, familiarize yourself with their criteria, and watch the video extract with these criteria in mind.

Activity 20   Yardsticks (3)

The assessment

After watching the sample of practice, it is time to make your assessment of the student's work in the light of the criteria you have agreed to use (these might be your own, or criteria devised by another group, if you are doing this as a large group exercise).

Individually, give a 'first impression' rating for *each* of the criteria, using these categories:

- very good
- good
- average
- poor
- very poor
- not possible to rate

In addition, *if you are in a group*, share your ratings to see what *similarities* and *differences* there are. If there are criteria which it was not possible to rate, discuss why.

Finally, discuss these two questions:

- Were the criteria useful in helping to assess the student's practice, and would you modify them in any way?
- With hindsight, are there other criteria which you would like to include?

Notes for practice teachers

A number of studies highlight lack of clear criteria as one of the difficulties in assessing practice competence (Brandon and Davies, 1979; Morrell, 1979; Syson and Baginsky, 1981). Each of the three principles below is designed to guide your assessment of individual students, and is demonstrated by the *Yardsticks* approach.

Assessing a student's readiness to practise: Three principles

Specific areas of practice

Before you can make a judgement about whether the student is ready to practise, you need to make a judgement about what *is* good practice. What will the student's practice be judged against?

If you were assessing a student who was learning to cook, you would look at different skills in cooking – from an ability to boil an egg (not that easy, actually) to competence with soufflés. In each dish, you would look for presentation and colour as well as taste and texture. You might inspect a collection of dishes, to see how the student balances a meal overall. You would also want to assess other aspects of these skills, such as kitchen hygiene, economical cooking, knowledge of nutrition and ability to work as part of a culinary team. 'Readiness to cook' is a composite ability which needs to be broken up into its constituent parts, while not losing sight of how they relate to each other. It is the same in social work.

Prior to the assessment event

It feels unfair if we are judged against standards which we did not know about.

A student cook who understands a 'good' boiled egg to be one with a firm white and a softish yolk will feel cheated if the egg is judged by different criteria. Aesthetics is a notoriously difficult area in which to find agreement (check your criteria for a 'good' cup of tea against the criteria of your student and your colleagues). However, if you know your colleague's criteria *before* you make it, you will know whether you have been successful. In other words: a minimum expectation is that you know what the criteria are, even if you are not in full agreement with them.

Collaboration with others

If you are the sole judge of good practice, there will be factors which you do not think about, and the ones you *do* include will be influenced by your own cultural bio-graphy (see Chapter 7).

As we saw with the simple case of a boiled egg or a cup of tea, criteria are not written on tablets of stone. It is important to check your notions of good practice with others, so that you can work out a 'triangulation' of opinions (see Chapter 3). If there is serious disagreement between you and the student about criteria for good practice in a particular area, it is crucial that this emerges before the assessment event, not after it.

In particular, it is important that the student takes part in developing the criteria. Establishing what is 'good' practice is where the twin features of learning and assess-ment meet, and students are more likely to be successful if they are in a position to *know* whether they have succeeded or not! The very act of discussing criteria for good practice aids the student's learning, because they are learning *why* they do, as well as *what* they do. This process helps to make assessment and learning congruent with each other.

Methods of assessment: Gathering evidence

These three principles are designed to provide a balance between objectivity and subjectivity in the assessment of the student. The *Yardsticks* approach provides an opportunity to develop relatively objective criteria from a subjective base. It helps to ensure that criteria are sensitive to the context of this particular student in this particular setting.

Despite the changing face of practice teaching, it seems that the main method of assessment, certainly in fieldwork settings, remains the judgements formulated in a one-to-one supervision session once a week (Williamson et al., 1989: 20). Reliance on one assessment method has great limitations – here are some other methods.

Sampling (assessment events)

The debate about assessment is often conducted between 'total assessment' (all of the student's work on placement is assessed) and 'sampling' (particular examples are taken for assessment at agreed times). In practice, all assessment is sampled; the distinction is whether the sample is implicit or explicit, *ad hoc* or planned.

In effect, 'total assessment' gives assessors licence to take any part of the student's practice at any time and include it as a sample of practice. In fact, it is impossible to include all the student's work, so total assessment becomes an implicit form of sampling. From the assessor's point of view, it is very flexible; but as an arbitrary activity, it can be oppressive to the assessed, and contributes little to the student's learning. What is called 'sampled assessment' is actually no more sampled than 'total assessment', but it is planned, timed and coordinated, so that the student knows which aspects of practice will be assessed at which times. We might refer to these as *assessment events*. This seems to be a fairer approach. Used flexibly, it should also include the opportunity for the assessor to make judgements about competence which require sampling over time (e.g. regular qualities of punctuality, reliability and consistency).

Direct observation and video work

Direct observation is a formal requirement of the Diploma in Social Work, and it has considerable advantages and some difficulties. See Chapter 18 (pages 148–9) for an approach to direct observation which links assessment with learning. You need to check with your programmes (both the student's DipSW course and the programme offering the Practice Teaching Award) whether video work counts as direct observation. There is guidance about using video on pages 149–51.

Client feedback

Client opinion as a way of assessing student competence is in its infancy. Despite the undoubted difficulties in this area, you and the student should consider it together. See Chapter 3; see also Doel and Shardlow (1993: 103–5), and Evans (1992: 48–50).

Student self-assessment

The *Yardsticks* approach has already indicated the value of involving students in developing criteria for good practice, so that they are judged by criteria of (partly) their own making. Who makes the judgement itself? In fact, there is no reason why the practice teacher and the student should not both make their own independent judgements, using the same criteria, and present these in the assessment documentation. Certainly, if the need for a second opinion arises, this approach will have been particularly useful (see Chapter 21).

The action techniques described in Chapter 16 as methods to aid the student's learning are also available as methods of gathering evidence for assessment (Sawdon, 1985). So far, we have been looking at methods of gathering evidence to make a judgement about competence. In Chapter 21, we will detail how you can present this evidence.

Rehearsing the assessment process

It is just as necessary to rehearse how to assess and be assessed as it is to rehearse how to do social work. Take the idea of a 'good cup of tea' (page 168) as a simple example of the process of developing criteria. Together with the student, and other colleagues if possible, look at the factors involved. It is a relatively simple area of life, and it is worth going through this process before looking at the parallels with developing criteria for social work practice.

The notion of competence must include a broader canvas than performance. Good-enough practice means a knowledge of why this practice is good or not good, as well as how to make it better. There is a balance to be achieved between an ability to analyse practice as good or poor, and an ability to *deliver* good-enough practice. Of course, there are parallels with your own assessment as a practice teacher for the Practice Teaching Award. An understanding of what constitutes good or poor teaching needs to be balanced by an ability to *carry out* good-enough practice teaching, with the facility to *demonstrate* good-enough practice teaching via a portfolio.

Intermittent assessment

Building on the notion of the assessment event described on page 148, it is helpful to think of assessments taking place at intervals throughout the placement (continual, as opposed to continuous, assessment). In this way, it is also possible to measure the incline of progress for the student.

An example of taking two 'readings' is to ask the student to make a note of their responses to an exercise like 'Boundaries' (in Doel and Shardlow, 1993: 23–4) early in the placement, and to revisit the exercise late in the placement to see how the student's views and practices have changed (or not) as a result of the learning which has taken place in the interim.

Selecting your sample

The *Yardsticks* approach to assessment – developing criteria for specific assessment events – is effective but time-consuming. Developing criteria in that methodical fashion for all the areas of the student's practice is not feasible, so how do you decide which samples to take and what other methods of assessment to use?

It helps if the requirements for the Diploma in Social Work are organized into clusters of learning. Each cluster, or unit, can be assessed separately. For example, the South Yorkshire programme has eighteen units of learning for Placement One (South

Yorkshire, 1993). This requires the student to demonstrate competence in eighteen areas of practice competence during their first placement, and the practice teacher must make opportunities available so that each of these areas can be tested. One assessment event can, of course, test more than one unit of practice.

Most programmes, including South Yorkshire's, have not yet set priorities between units, whose titles might vary from 'Power and Oppression' to 'Time Management', and there is much work to be done to develop schemes for sampling in a coherent way. *Yardsticks* would be time-consuming even with the requirements clustered into eighteen units. In the absence of a programme-wide scheme for sampling, you should not be expected to create your own; however, it is important to demonstrate your understanding of these issues (even if only to point to the difficulties of your present methods of making assessments) and to show an ability to use planned sampling of the *Yardsticks* variety at least once.

Standards and CCETSW's statement of requirements

Programmes have interpreted CCETSW's requirements for the Diploma in Social Work (CCETSW, 1991b) in different ways, and this will no doubt be true of the 1995 Review also. There were about 120 Requirements in the 1991 document, and the 1995 Review details six core competences:

- communicate and engage
- promote and enable
- assess and plan
- intervene
- work in organizations
- develop professional competence

The 1995 Review also sets out twenty-six Practice Requirements (examples of these are: form and develop working relationships with children, adults, families, carers and groups; work in partnership to assess and review people's needs, rights, risks, strengths, responsibilities and resources; contribute to the management of packages of care, support, protection and control). The Review states that 'in order to provide evidence that they have achieved the six core competences students will have to demonstrate that they have: met practice requirements; integrated social work values; acquired and applied knowledge; and critically analysed their practice in the light of knowledge and values' (CCETSW, 1995: 3). As a practice teacher, you need to be familiar with the way the student's programme interprets the Practice Requirements (via the practice curriculum or placement handbook).

It is always difficult to know how specific to be when setting standards. Some programmes have developed very specific indicators, both positive and negative, in relation to given criteria. The former CQSW programme at Leicester University provides an example of this kind, with a series of positive and negative indicators for inputs and outcomes. For example:

D.   Ability to work within the agency

Criterion	Positive indicators	Negative indicators
	Input	
16 Ability to organize a workload and to decide on priorities.	Consistent evidence of forethought and planning for contact with clients; priorities are ordered in regard to seriousness and to his/her client's needs rather than his/her own interests; client contact is organized by appointment where possible; appropriate intensity of contact is assessed.	Cases are undifferentiated as to seriousness by the student; little importance is given to planning; there is little attempt to 'weight' cases appropriately.
	Outcome	
	Contacts are invariably carried out as planned; serious cases are never neglected; importance is given to agency rules about the frequency of client contact; a flexible balance between organization of work and responsiveness to crises is achieved.	Serious cases are sometimes neglected; there is little evidence of needs of cases being converted into thoughtful action; inconsistency in client contact.

(From Curnock and Prins, 1982: 525)

As a practice teacher, you should know whether the student's DipSW programme sets different standards for successive phases of the course. Are standards for a student in the first placement at a lower level than for a student on a final placement? Is the student assessed in different areas of competence from one placement to another, and is any self-referencing system required (i.e. where the student's *progress* is measured)?

Most programmes include individualized learning objectives set out in a Learning Agreement (see Chapter 5), but it is important to relate these to the programme's objectives, as detailed in the placement curriculum. Ultimately, standards arise out of the 'consensus within the community of assessors' (Evans, 1992: 37), and these will change as the context of social work practice changes.

The practice teaching portfolio

Your portfolio should demonstrate your ability as a practice teacher to make an assessment of practice competence, using a variety of methods. You should make reference to the different methods you have used, but in general it helps to give more detail about one particular method and how you used it. An appraisal of the method – its advantages and disadvantages – also demonstrates your ability to use it appropriately.

Example 20

Shula, a practice teacher, discussed the *Yardsticks* approach with Simone, a student, and they both agreed to use it at least once, early in the placement. The particular area of practice which they chose was 'working with difference', which was relevant throughout the practice curriculum, with a particular focus in the 'Power and Oppression' unit.

Shula and Simone developed separate, independent criteria as a start, and discussed how their individual biographies led to differences and similarities in each of their sets of criteria (in itself a good model for working with difference). They negotiated a mutual set of criteria, and Shula included this in her portfolio, along with the individual sets. She described how the criteria were used to assess a piece of Simone's practice later that same week. Her portfolio briefly described one modification they made to the criteria in the light of this run-through, and their separate judgements about Simone's practice (in fact, Shula and Simone had made very similar assessments).

Shula mentioned in her portfolio how Simone used the *Yardsticks* approach (unsupervised by Shula) later in the placement, and Shula included this as an example of student self-assessment in the assessment document at the completion of the placement.

21 Ready to practise?

About Activity 21   Ready or not?

Ready or not? is a four-part exercise which is best treated as a piece of practice teaching 'soap opera'. It helps you to think about the factors which influence your assessment judgements, and this is especially true of events and suspicions whose significance it is difficult to gauge at the time.

Purpose

This chapter focuses on the difficulties practice teachers encounter when they are considering recommending a 'fail'. Failure is reframed as 'not yet ready to practise'; this does not remove the sting of the decision, but it helps to bring some clarity to the process of making it.

Method

Ready or not? is best discussed in small groups of three to six practice teachers.

- Each of the four parts of the *Ready or not?* activity should be available on *separate* sheets of paper, so that they can be given to your group to discuss at intervals. *Do not read Part 2 until you have finished discussing Part 1, etc.*
- Follow the instructions on each of the four pages, with the suggested time limits at the bottom of each page.
- If a number of small groups are completing the exercise, come back together to discuss what each group learned from the activity (*not* to compare notes about what they would have done at each stage).

Variations

Ready or not? can be completed individually, but it benefits from the discussions and support of a small group. One of the learning points to be drawn from this kind of activity is the support gained from a regular group of practice teachers who gather together to discuss exactly these kinds of difficulties.

The issues raised by *Ready or not?* are not specific to the setting of this activity, and most people can draw parallels with their own work setting. However, you may choose to re-write the soap opera to fit more closely with your own work.

For more consideration of the notion of 'readiness to practise' see Marsh and Triseliotis (1992).

Activity 21   Ready or not? (1)

This activity can be completed individually, but it is best done in a group.

Consider yourselves as a group of practice teachers meeting to discuss progress in connection with students you have on placement. It is the first meeting soon after the beginning of a student placement and you discuss the following situation.

The student arrived late on the first morning of the placement, but apologized profusely. He said that he had 'domestic problems', but they had been sorted out. However, he also turned up late for a team meeting, and one of the clerk-receptionists tells you he forgot to sign a letter of appointment to see a client. Smiling knowingly, she also says that he has been receiving a lot of phone calls from a woman. It is nearly a week into the placement, and the first practice teaching session is due.

- What course of action would the group of practice teachers advise at this stage?
- Make a brief note on flip-chart paper of the options discussed and any agreed course of action.

Allow ten minutes, including two to three minutes to write notes on the flip-chart, before reading Part 2.

Activity 21   Ready or not? (2)

These are the developments since the last meeting of the practice teachers' group.

The student has told you about the recent death of his father and the demands which his mother has been making on him, including telephoning him at work. He apologizes and says that the situation is under control now and he does not expect the situation to interfere with his work.

The student's time-keeping improves for a week, but then there is a morning when he does not come in to the office, and the receptionist is unable to say when he is expected back. She says she is 'not doing any covering up for that student of yours', and that she 'doesn't like his off-hand attitude', but she won't elaborate.

In addition, you learn from a colleague that the student was half an hour late for a case discussion in another agency, to which he had been invited as an observer. You subsequently receive a telephone call from the person who chaired that discussion (a Social Services team leader) to complain about his manner. The team leader says: 'We were discussing what to do when a Schedule One offender is released from prison when your student made it clear that he thought the offender's wife, a client of our Department, should have been present at the discussion. I had understood that he was there as an observer.'

A colleague mentions what useful ideas the student expressed at a planning meeting for a young offenders' group. You observed the student conducting an office interview yesterday, and you were impressed by his ability to engage with the client and structure the interview.

- You are now just over two weeks into the placement and discussing this situation with the practice teachers' group. What advice does the group give at this stage?
- Make a brief note on flip-chart paper of the options discussed and any agreed course of action.

Allow fifteen minutes, including three to four minutes to write notes on the flip-chart, before reading Part 3.

Activity 21   Ready or not? (3)

These are the developments since the last meeting of the practice teachers' group.

The student has told you that he is allowed half a day a week study time, and that accounts for his absence from the office. He had assumed that the office was aware of this – 'I thought that was your responsibility.' He feels the team leader in Social Services had been unreasonable in the way the case discussion had been chaired, and he agreed that he just doesn't 'hit it off with the receptionist'.

At the end of the session, you are in a hurry to get to another appointment. As you get up to leave, the student tells you that his course tutor will be in touch to discuss the implications of a possible accusation of plagiarism in one of his essays. The student says this is untrue, but he may have used some of the notes he took from his reading and transcribed them into the essay without realizing they were, in fact, direct quotes. If it is a mistake, 'I guess I'll have to re-write the essay.'

Your colleague who has been planning the young offenders' group has asked if your student can join as a third co-leader, because: 'He's got such a lot to contribute and worked exceptionally well with the lads when he went as a helper on an outing.' You bump into Delroy, one of the young offenders in the group. He is 16, but looks a lot older, and you know his family well. He says that your student is 'the best ever – gave me his home phone number if I ever needed help when the office is closed and he even bought me a p—. . .' Delroy stops himself, but you suspect he was going to say 'pint'. 'Don't say I said anything, will you, I don't want to get him into trouble; he's really helping me,' says Delroy.

- Luckily, there is another meeting of the practice teachers in your agency to discuss what should happen next.
- Make a brief note on flip-chart paper of the options discussed and any agreed course of action.

Allow fifteen minutes, including three to four minutes to write notes on the flip-chart, before reading Part 4.

Activity 21   Ready or not? (4)

This time, consider how the following new different pieces of information would influence the outcome.

4a

The student, Colin, is a white 24-year-old, not long graduated from City New University. Colin has put 'Use of a Written Agreement with Delroy' on the agenda for the practice teaching session. He explains that he had indeed bought Delroy a pint of beer, but that it had been part of a written agreement with him to get him off drugs: 'It seemed reasonable to trade in a more serious drug for a less serious one, and it's working. Delroy's a different person these days.' The co-leaders of the group agree that there has been a remarkable change in Delroy, and give credit to the student. They knew Colin had planned to use a written agreement, but had not seen the contents.

4b

The student, Dave, is a black 24-year-old, not long graduated from City New University. He says that he has experienced a lot of antagonism in the office (though not from you), and feels that this is definitely due to racism. He feels that this, coupled with all the problems at home following the death of his father, makes for unfair pressure on him. He says that he gets no complaints from clients and thinks he is doing good work with them, but he is considering submitting a grievance about the racism in the office and would like your advice.

- Make a brief note of the course of action which the group would advise in each of these events and the reasons.
- Prepare a flip-chart page summarizing what the group has learnt from this exercise. Bring this flip-chart paper back to the main group, ready for feedback.

Allow thirty minutes, including five minutes to write notes on the flip-chart.

Notes for practice teachers

Gathering evidence of competence is a different activity from helping students to learn, and this can be a difficult transition for practice teachers. In *Ready or not?*, you had the strength and guidance of a group of practice teachers to make this transition, and it is important to build this kind of support network for yourself.

Ready to practise?

The reluctance of practice teachers and tutors to fail students has been well documented (e.g. Baird, 1991), yet most people can think of a colleague whom they would not have passed for practice. Or would they? The decision of whether to recommend that a person is ready to practise is tough, with important consequences, and *Ready or not?* highlights the fact that it is not acceptable to make a judgement without being clear about the evidence on which it is based. There are many reasons why it is difficult to make the judgement that a student is not ready to practise:

- awareness of the consequences for adult social work students
- developing a closeness to the student and an understanding of their difficulties
- lack of confidence, in the absence of a general measure of good-enough practice
- lack of confidence, for fear that your own judgement is culture-specific
- lack of sufficient rigour in the assessment process
- difficulties pinpointing the evidence to back up your concerns
- lack of support from others (college tutor, etc.)
- fear that the student's failure reflects on your own teaching abilities
- 'all-or-nothing' effect of a pass/fail choice

What to do about this?

Creating an open assessment climate (Chapter 19) and developing clear criteria for competence (Chapter 20) will not make the problem go away, but they should help you to feel confident that the placement has been fair to the student, and guide your judgement about precisely why the student is not ready to practise.

Traditionally, the language of assessment has used words like 'pass' and 'fail'. This is unhelpful if we are considering a person's readiness to practise. Each student will have areas of practice where they are more ready than others, and some students will not be ready at all in certain areas. It is unrealistic to make a single judgement on the whole of a student's competence; better to assess the student's readiness to practise in different areas, or 'units', of practice learning. Programmes which have clustered the learning into units offer practice assessors an opportunity to make these more sophisticated, fine-tuned judgements (South Yorkshire, 1993).

In Chapters 18 and 20 we have seen how 'total assessment' has meant that each sneeze and eyeblink of the student's placement can, in theory, be selected as an assessable moment. Assessment events, planned at regular intervals during the placement, provide a focus for the assessment (see page 148). These events give yardsticks to measure progress – or lack of it – during the placement, and they train the student into an understanding of what 'readiness to practise' means.

Second opinions

Making a judgement about a student at the margins of competence requires considerable confidence. One way to increase confidence is to gather other people's opinions. Note that this gives you the confidence to make a judgement which is likely to be accurate, not necessarily the confidence to confirm your own first judgement.

Chapter 3 looked at measuring your own competence as a practice teacher, using the metaphor of the Sea of Practice Teaching (page 17). A similar framework can be used to consider the student's practice competence, to be found somewhere in the re-named 'Sea of Practice Competence'. (See the triangulation model in Shardlow and Doel, 1993b.)

CCETSW Paper 30 made second opinions mandatory in some circumstances:

> (i)   the practice teacher's assessment recommendations must stand in their own right as recommendations to the Programme Assessment Board. Where the practice teacher considers that a student's practice is likely to be on the margins or lead to a fail decision, a second opinion should be sought from another practice teacher. (CCETSW, 1991b, para. 3.4.4.5)

However, CCETSW did not suggest the process by which the second opinion should be sought. Clearly, it is easier to ask for second opinions if they have already been incorporated into the assessment process as good practice, not just when there are doubts, though you may wish to consider gathering a second opinion from somebody who is reasonably independent of the placement. You need to know before a placement begins about your DipSW programme regulations and guidelines concerning who should be approached to give a second opinion, and how that process should be managed.

Making judgements about readiness to practise cannot be divorced from the notion of culture (see Chapter 9). Your gender, race, class and other aspects of your biography all influence your view of good-enough practice. A second opinion from people with diverse cultural biographies, some of which are similar to the student's, is an essential element of a fair assessment system. In the late 1970s, at the conclusion of her CCETSW study on assessment, Hayward (1979: 183) advocated a team approach to assessment, with students, practice teachers and college teachers 'clarifying the purpose, nature and content of the formal assessment conducted on the course'. The need to broaden the involvement in student assessment remains.

Evans (1992: 10–11) points to the difficulties which the division in the assessment of practice between academic and agency settings can produce. The DipSW is intended to increase collaboration between these two arms of the assessment process, but collaboration often means more work, and may not always be welcomed. (How do you feel about giving second opinions about students' class assignments?) The support of the tutor is important when making a case that a student is not ready to practise; that support is likely to be more forthcoming if your detailed case is backed with a second opinion.

Presenting evidence

Chapter 20 focused on how to *gather* evidence, illustrated by developing criteria for assessment purposes. The next stage is how to *present* the evidence. A major factor is: *Who is the principal author of the evidence which is presented?*

Teacher-authored or student-authored?

The balance of contributions by practice teacher and student to the assessment documentation has been variable. The CQSW relied heavily on the final assessment report, authored primarily by the practice teacher. CSS programmes generally placed more emphasis on student-authored assignments. College-based assessment is almost entirely based on student-authored work. The DipSW places a greater emphasis on direct observation as a method of gathering evidence, but there is less guidance about how this evidence should be presented for examination.

Doel and Shardlow (1989) developed the notion of a portfolio of student-authored practice assignments to examine practice ability on placements. The project was based on the premise that the best way to assess students' practice competence was to have them present it themselves. The notion of a practice assignment was found to give focus to the assessment process and to have a beneficial effect on the student's learning. On the down side, assignments had the potential to miss areas of competence, and some participants in the project found them time-consuming. In general, the students were more enthusiastic about practice assignments, the practice teachers less so.

Whenever students do present their own work, it is important they have the opportunity to present work in their first language (oral or written), with translation facilities for the assessors if necessary. You might want to consider this principle for yourself as a practice teacher, too.

Writing the assessment report

The practice teacher's assessment report remains a major instrument for presenting evidence of the student's abilities for the DipSW, as for the CQSW. Guidelines for writing the report on the student's practice competence are now common and are usually included in the practice teaching handbook for the DipSW programme. The guidelines may be more or less specific; some have tended to follow the pattern of National Vocational Qualification schedules, with long lists of tick-box items. They sometimes include positive and negative indicators to help the assessor make a judgement, and there may be a scale, asking the practice teacher to fine-tune the assessment – in other words: was the particular learning objective very well achieved, well achieved, reasonably achieved, not achieved, or not attempted? These checklists are often very numerous indeed (see page 172).

At the other end of the continuum from the 'telephone directory approach' are guidelines which are general and open-ended. These may be framed as broad questions which the practice teacher is invited to consider in connection with different areas of practice competence (South Yorkshire, 1993).

Both approaches have advantages and disadvantages. Indicators help focus assessments, but they may overshadow the learning, as student and teacher focus on a large body of outcomes. Open-ended assessment questions give space to the practice teacher and student to tailor the assessment to the particular placement setting and experience, but may provide less guarantee of a common standard of assessment over the whole programme. Paradoxically, the more specific the curriculum for practice learning, the more open-ended the assessment schedule can be, because it is tied to a clear base. Some factors to consider when writing the report:

Equal opportunities and the student input

How much evidence is the student expected to collect? In other words, to what extent is your report balanced by evidence presented by the student? For example, in class settings, students present all their own work for examination.

The more the student's work is mediated via the practice teacher's judgements, as recorded in the assessment report, the more power it gives to the practice teacher at the student's expense. Black, female views of competence might vary from white, male views (Shakeshaft, 1990), and it is an important aspect of equal opportunities to have different perspectives included in any assessment of ability.

What kind of evidence have you gathered to support your judgements?

If you have made regular use of feedback techniques (Chapter 10) and have employed a variety of methods to collect samples of the student's practice (Chapters 3, 18, 19, 20), you should be in a good position to provide a rounded picture of that practice – what we might call the 'shape' of the student's practice competence. For example, you know that if you look at a coin from just one angle it might appear either as a broad, flat disc or as a thin, serrated edge. These two shapes bear little relation to each other, or to the thing you know as a coin, until you can see it from many different angles. So it is with the student's practice competence.

A compilation of many assessment events

The final report should not be the occasion when you make your final assessment decision. It is the time when you bring together the many different assessments which you have already made during the course of the placement. If you have had doubts and concerns, these should have been registered before the compilation of the report, with calls for a second opinion if necessary.

The report does not signify one assessment, but a multitude of separate yet connected assessments. The student will most likely have shown strengths in some areas and weaknesses in others; indeed, a student might demonstrate strong readiness to practise in some areas of the practice curriculum whilst failing to demonstrate this readiness in others. The development of a practice curriculum with specific units of learning means that it is possible to make judgements on different aspects of practice learning, rather than having to pronounce on a general 'pass' or 'fail'. We have already seen how the all-or-nothing effect can lead to assessors swallowing their concerns and recommending a 'pass', even when they have serious doubts.

Proof of competence, not proof of incompetence

In terms of the assessment, the student should be assumed 'not yet ready to practise' until there is *evidence of readiness*, rather than assuming the student is ready in the *absence of proof of unreadiness*. This is an important distinction, since it can mean that the placement has sometimes failed in its role towards the student – for example, when there has not been an opportunity for the student to demonstrate ability in a certain area. In these circumstances, it may be necessary for the student to carry out further work on placement, or carry parts of the assessment to the next placement, if this is possible. Simulations may provide indications of readiness – for instance, if a trainee pilot performs excellently in the flight simulator, can it be assumed that this guarantees competence in actual flight? The answer is 'probably'.

It is important to know *before* the placement begins what opportunities the DipSW programme provides for a student to complete additional work, in the event of you recommending that there is a part of the practice learning where you do not yet consider the student ready to practise.

The practice teaching portfolio

Your portfolio should include examples of your written assessments on students (usually assessment reports on two different students). Focus on one of these reports to describe how you arrived at your decisions about whether the student was ready to practise. Did you have the same confidence (or lack of it) in all aspects of the student's practice?

If you have been in a position to recommend a 'fail' or 'not yet ready to practise', include an evaluation of this in your portfolio.

Example 21

Marilyn described in her portfolio the way her concerns about some aspects of Barry's practice developed. During work together early in the placement, she observed practices which she feared might create dependency in clients, and her discussions about this with Barry seemed to have only a small influence on his work. She discussed his strengths, too, because there were many areas of practice where he functioned very well.

Towards the middle of the placement, Marilyn requested a second opinion from a male practice teacher regarding this one aspect of Barry's practice. The three of them developed criteria for good practice for the ability to *help a person without creating dependency*. These criteria were used against an audio tape of Barry with a client, and – in addition – the second practice teacher went to interview the same client later in the placement.

Marilyn described in her portfolio how her final judgement, backed by the second opinion, was that Barry was (just!) ready to practise in this area, but she was convinced that the coaching which Barry had received via the assessment process had helped his learning considerably. In this particular instance, the clear assessment procedure helped to draw the student above the margin and to alert the next practice teacher to look for continued progress; it could just as easily have pinpointed Barry's position below the margin.

The Portfolio

22 The portfolio

At the end of each of the twenty-one chapters in this book, we have given examples of how you might demonstrate your practice teaching abilities in a portfolio. This chapter explores in more detail how you might prepare and present your portfolio of work for the Practice Teaching Award. There are parallels between this activity and the presentation of students' work for examination discussed in the previous chapter.

What is a portfolio?

A portfolio is a representation of your abilities as a practice teacher. It requires thought and skill to transform what is essentially a 'three-dimensional' activity into a 'two-dimensional' format – practice teaching is an inter-active, dynamic process, whereas the portfolio is a static 2-D snapshot of your work.

The portfolio reflects a combination of two abilities:

● your ability to teach social work practice
● your ability to demonstrate your ability to teach social work practice

The chapters in this book have helped you to develop your skills in practice teaching, but it is also necessary to develop skills in gathering and presenting evidence of your work as a practice teacher. You could be an excellent practice teacher, but fail to demonstrate this or neglect to provide sufficient evidence in a portfolio. This chapter consolidates the learning from the examples at the conclusion of each of the previous chapters.

The requirements for the Practice Teaching Award

The requirements for the Practice Teaching Award are set out in CCETSW Paper 26.3 (CCETSW, 1991a), *Improving Standards in Practice Learning*, and are being reviewed in CCETSW Paper 26.4 (forthcoming, 1995). You should make sure that you have a copy of these documents, which spell out how agencies are approved for practice learning, how practice teachers are accredited, the requirements of the Practice Teaching Award, the contents of the portfolio, and the requirements for approved practice teacher training programmes.

CCETSW outlined fourteen requirements for the Practice Teaching Award in Paper 26.3 (CCETSW, 1991a: 10). These covered no more than one page, and were written in very general language – for example, the third requirement was to demonstrate an ability to *help students to relate theory to practice*. Paper 26.4 (Draft 3 is available at the time of going to press) suggests five units of competence: values, management, teaching, assessment and reflective practice. Each unit contains a number of elements.

Each practice teaching programme provides guidance about how it has put CCETSW's requirements into operation. This book reflects the South Yorkshire/ N.E. Midlands Partnership curriculum, with seven modules of learning, each one presented as three units in this book.

Make sure that you have regulations and guidelines available for the particular programme with which you are registered. These are some of the questions you will want answered:

- What needs to go into the portfolio?
- How should the portfolio be presented?
- How long after registration can I submit the portfolio?
- When are the submission dates and when does the Examination Board meet?
- What opportunity do I have to re-submit my portfolio if necessary?
- What support will I get from my agency? (time made available/direct observation of practice teaching, etc.)
- Who will write the report of direct observation of my practice teaching?

Start gathering your evidence now

Whether your plans are clear or vague about when or whether you want to present a portfolio for the Practice Teaching Award, it is worth collecting evidence immediately.

The first step is to find out how your programme asks you to organize your portfolio. Get the ring-binder which will house your portfolio, and divide it into the sections advised by your practice teaching programme. You may also want to include other items at this stage, such as previous student reports, if you have them.

As you begin to accumulate ideas, incidents, articles and the like, make a note of them and collect them in the relevant section of your portfolio. If you have a student currently on placement, there will be no shortage of material to jot down; the difficulty will be keeping pace with the amount of material and finding time to make a note as soon as possible. Even if you are not currently teaching a student, ideas and activities will come to mind which it is worth recording briefly. What started as an empty ring-binder with card dividers will gradually change into a portfolio, as you become more familiar with what to look for and how to relate it to the different sections.

This method of gathering evidence means that the final job of presenting the portfolio is one of editing and consolidating existing materials. Not a small task, but less daunting than starting from scratch. You will feel more at home with the portfolio, and your materials and examples are likely to be more vivid because you have recorded them at the time, rather than through the haze of memory.

One of the aims of this book has been to help you collect evidence as you progress, so that your learning and your gathering evidence of this learning go hand in hand.

Tips on how to present your portfolio

If you have very clear ideas about how to present your work, this section may seem a bit basic. Nevertheless, it is worth learning from these experiences of receiving and reading many portfolios:

- A loose-leaf ring-binder format is the most flexible format. (The programme with which you enrol may have its own folder to use.) It should be large enough and strong enough to take the contents (remember to include space for a video if the programme requires this).
- Make sure that your portfolio can be quickly identified (name and agency on the spine of the binder, etc.).
- Include a clear contents page at the start of the portfolio, to help assessors find their way around quickly.
- Use coloured dividers to separate the different sections.
- Clear plastic wallets for back-to-back pages will protect the individual sheets, if your agency will meet the expense.
- The video tape should be secured within the portfolio. A zipped plastic wallet (with reinforced holes for the ring-binder down the edge) is better than stapling an ordinary plastic wallet.

Although the medium is not the message, the quality of presentation has an undoubted influence on how the quality of your content will be perceived. If assessors are able to go straight into a well-organized, clearly-presented portfolio, this is an important first step to their understanding what you have to say.

Cross-referencing

As well as how much and what to put in your portfolio, there is also the question of *where* to put it. It helps to think yourself into the shoes of the person or persons who will be reading your portfolio – the assessors. Is it appropriate to include the actual exercise you have just described and evaluated? Certainly, it can help the assessors to understand your commentary if they have access to the exercise itself. Consider including this kind of item in an appendix, and make sure you cross-reference it, so that the assessors can make the relevant connections. You may want to refer to this same item from a different section in the portfolio, too.

Weeding out your portfolio is as important as filling it. It is tempting to include every policy document, training exercise and photocopied article you can lay your hands on, but this only reduces the impact of those items which really are important. Each time you include an item in your portfolio, consider whether it is really necessary (how does it illustrate your practice teaching?), and discard it if it is not.

Prioritizing what goes into your portfolio makes the assessor's job easier, and helps you to highlight the main points about your practice teaching.

Try to arrange for your portfolio to be proofread (you might enter a reciprocal arrangement with a practice teacher going through the same process).

Use specific examples

The portfolio is not an academic document, so it should not read like a collection of essays. Reference it with examples of your actual practice, rather than lots of texts and articles (though it is fine to include some references to these).

Another pitfall is the tendency to give statements of good intention, to the exclusion of what you *actually* did. It is OK to have an idea of what good practice teaching means, but if your portfolio is shot through with 'woulds', 'shoulds' and 'oughts', it is a strong sign that you are relying on good intention to the detriment of real examples.

Above all, the assessor of your portfolio is looking for examples – good, bad or indifferent – of your practice teaching. Make your examples as specific as possible. A detailed illustration is worth more than a hundred generalizations. You should aim to have a specific example for the areas outlined in this book, though one composite example might illustrate more than one module (e.g. the links between the examples of Shula's work with Simone on pages 151, 161 and 173).

Sometimes it helps to use contrasting examples:

> With student A in situation X, I used this particular method of teaching because...
> While with student B in situation Y, I used an alternative method because...
> (or, with student A in situation Z, etc....)
> and what worked best was...
> and what worked least was...
> and my main learning as a practice teacher from this experience has been...

Reflective practice teaching

It is natural to want to present your best work when it is being assessed for examination. On a driving test, you do not want to hit the kerb, fail to stop at a junction or give wrong answers to the *Highway Code* questions. The driving test is very much about 'right' and 'wrong' ways of doing things – the learner wants to get as close as possible to an agreed ideal of perfect driving.

Social work practice, and practice teaching, do not have this same kind of agreed 'ideal'. There are better and worse practices, but not such clear ideas of right and wrong. Moreover, good practice includes the ability to be self-reflective. In other words, good teaching is demonstrated when the practice teacher is able to look at things that did not work and to learn from them.

You should not feel obliged to present examples of glittering practice teaching, or to shine up the humdrum. The portfolio is not intended to put you on the spot, or ask you to justify your teaching. Avoid long, narrative descriptions of what happened, or rationalizations after the event; the portfolio is an opportunity for you to *evaluate* your own practice teaching.

It will help to keep these three questions in mind, each time you are presenting an example of practice teaching in your portfolio – in relation to this example of my practice teaching:

- What was I doing and why?
- What worked and what didn't work?
- What have I learned from this?

If you are able to answer these questions and to address them in the portfolio, you are likely to be presenting reflective, self-evaluative work.

The video and written evaluation

Earlier, we described the difficulties of presenting a 3-D activity like practice teaching in a 2-D format like a portfolio. This problem is not confined to practice teaching. If you were to assess a baker's ability to bake bread, you would find a photograph of the loaf, with a self-evaluation, not quite the same as the smell and taste of a freshly-baked sample. Additional reports from experienced bakers who had tasted the bread themselves would go some way towards satisfying you, but not quite all the way.

A video is the nearest that the assessors can get to 'tasting' your actual practice. Despite the accepted limitations of video (the difficulties in setting up the equipment, the nervousness that some people experience being filmed, etc.), it is an important piece of the jigsaw for the assessor. Even if your programme does not require one, think about including a video of your practice teaching.

The video should be taken from one of your regular practice teaching sessions; if you can video a number of sessions, you have more to choose from when it comes to selecting an extract. It is a good idea to limit the excerpt to between ten and fifteen minutes, with a brief description of the context for the extract in a written evaluation to accompany the video (see below). It helps the assessor if you wind the video so that it is ready to show at the beginning of the extract, with the opening and closing dialogue transcribed at the start of the written analysis (this confirms the start of the clip for assessors, and lets them know when it is over).

The video is incomplete without the written evaluation. This is what gives the video its context, and it enables the assessor to focus on your ability to evaluate your own teaching, using the video as illustrative material. Assessors look for evidence of good-enough practice teaching in the video itself, but it is your ability to evaluate your practice teaching (using the video extract as an illustration) and how you have *learned* from this which is of particular significance. The written analysis is where you can demonstrate this self-evaluation and learning (the trigger questions on page 192 should help).

The hints on using video to teach students (Chapter 18, pages 149–51) are also relevant to the use of video for your practice teaching portfolio.

The project

Some portfolios require the candidate to present work in a particular area of practice teaching, in the form of a project. This may use a number of different media (in other words, not necessarily in a written format).

The term 'project' can sound rather grand, but this is misleading. The best approach to the project is to think about what aspect of practice teaching you find especially interesting and would like to develop in some more detail. Think of the project as an opportunity to develop this interest further.

Examples of project areas include (this is by no means a comprehensive list):

1   Modifying or developing the practice curriculum to fit your particular setting

–   One candidate developed a number of modules of learning which were specific to his work in an alcohol advisory agency.

2   New materials or adaptations of materials to add to the practice teaching 'library' of methods and activities

–   Three candidates collaborated to make a series of video triggers to be used by other practice teachers to illustrate different kinds of interaction in a practice teaching session. Together they scripted three role-plays, allocated parts, videoed the role-plays and wrote brief accompanying notes for practice teachers using the video (see 'Shared work' below).

3   A particular sequence in the placement

–   One candidate developed an orientation package to use with students starting placements with her. As well as the details of the orientation programme, she included an evaluation of how it had worked, with revisions suggested by a student.

4   An agency policy document on practice teaching

–   One candidate developed a policy document concerning arrangements and resources for practice teaching in her agency. This was timed alongside the process of the agency gaining approval for practice teaching from CCETSW.

Shared work

Evidence of collaborative work in your portfolio is usually welcomed. However, because the Practice Teaching Award is awarded to you as an individual, rather than a 'team prize', it is important that you are able to demonstrate individual competence. In other words, if you are presenting joint materials, make sure the assessors can distinguish the nature of your own particular contribution.

In the example in item 2 in the list above, the completed video and notes were the same in each of the three candidates' portfolios, but they supplemented this with a description of their own particular contributions to the process.

The report of a practice assessor

The portfolio is a collection of different kinds of evidence to demonstrate your abilities as a practice teacher.

So far, we have described these methods of presenting this evidence:

- *Self-report*   your own descriptions and evaluations of your practice teaching, with an emphasis on your ability to be specific and reflective
- *Materials*   inclusion of selected materials which you use to aid your teaching (these might be borrowed materials, modified from existing materials, or self-generated), with an emphasis on being selective, so that the materials you choose to include in the portfolio have a greater impact
- *Video and written evaluation*   an excerpt from a regular practice teaching session with a student, accompanied by a written analysis to demonstrate what you have learned from observing your own practice teaching
- *Project*   a piece of work which shows a particular area of interest in practice teaching and your commitment to continuing your development as a practice teacher

A further piece of important evidence comes from somebody who is experienced as a practice teacher and who has directly witnessed you practice teaching with a student. This person is able to make an informed comment and judgement on your work, which is very helpful for the assessor of your portfolio.

The most helpful arrangement from your point of view is if you can have regular contact with a practice mentor, who can help your learning as a practice teacher as well as providing an evaluative report for your portfolio (there are links with the model for direct observation described in Chapter 18).

As a minimum, you should get together with the person who has agreed to observe your practice teaching, so that you can agree the groundrules. You both need to develop criteria by which your practice teaching session will be judged (again, there are links with the *Yardsticks* approach described in Chapter 20). During the course of one observation, the observer cannot be expected to make comment on the whole range of practice teaching skills required for the Award, so the observer needs to know what particular aspects of your teaching you hope the session will demonstrate.

The observer's report should use specific examples to illustrate the points being made.

Summary of handy hints

- Build your portfolio gradually, gathering evidence as you go along.
- Make the presentation of your portfolio 'user-friendly' for the assessors.
- Be selective in what you include; cross-reference where this helps.
- Keep examples specific and relevant.
- Avoid generalizations, statements of good intent and 'essays'.
- Concentrate on self-evaluation, not self-justification.

- Focus on your ability to learn, not just your ability to teach.
- Include examples of things that did not work – they often illuminate your learning more than things that did work.
- Ask someone to proofread your portfolio before you submit it.

CCETSW have published a guide to preparing portfolios in post-qualifying studies in general, not just for practice teaching (Doel and Shardlow, 1995).

Bibliography

Ahmad, Bandana (1990), *Black Perspectives in Social Work*, Birmingham: Venture Press. (Chapter 8)

Ahmed, Shama, Hallett, Christine, Statham, Daphne and Watt, Shantu (1988), 'A Code of Practice', *Social Work Education*, 7 (2): 7–8. (Chapters 8 and 19)

Baird, Peter (1991), 'The Proof of the Pudding: A study of client views of student practice competence', *Issues in Social Work Education*, 10 (1 & 2): 24–50. (Chapters 3, 7 and 21)

Barbour, Rosaline S. (1984), 'Social Work Education: Tackling the theory–practice dilemma', *British Journal of Social Work*, 14 (6): 557–78. (Chapter 15)

Bogo, Marion and Vayda, Elaine (1987), *The Practice of Field Instruction in Social Work*, Toronto: University of Toronto Press. (Chapters 1, 6, 15 and 16)

Brandes, Donna and Ginnis, Paul (1992), *A Guide to Student-Centred Learning*, Hemel Hempstead: Simon and Schuster Education (first published 1986). (Chapters 2 and 12)

Brandon, John and Davies, Martin (1979), 'The Limits of Competence in Social Work: The assessment of marginal students in social work education', *British Journal of Social Work*, 9 (3): 295–347. (Chapter 20)

Brummer, Nadine (1988), 'Cross-Cultural Assessment: Issues facing white teachers and black students', *Social Work Education*, 7 (2): 3–6. (Chapter 7)

Burgess, Hilary (1992), *Problem-led Learning for Social Work: The Enquiry and Action Approach*, London: Whiting and Birch. (Chapter 14)

Butler, Barbara and Elliott, Doreen (1985), *Teaching and Learning for Practice*, Community Care Practice Handbooks, Aldershot: Gower. (Chapters 1, 6, 13 and 16)

CCETSW (1986), *Three Years and Different Routes*, Paper 20.6, London: Central Council for Education and Training in Social Work. (Chapter 13)

CCETSW (1991a), *Improving Standards in Practice Learning: Requirements and Guidance for the Approval of Agencies and the Accreditation and Training of Practice Teachers*, Paper 26.3, London: Central Council for Education and Training in Social Work. (Chapters 5, 6 and 22)

CCETSW (1991b), *Requirements and Regulations for the Diploma in Social Work*, Paper 30, London: Central Council for Education and Training in Social Work. (Chapters 6, 8, 13, 18, 20 and 21)

CCETSW/OLF (1993), *Learning Good Practice in Community Care: A Handbook for Practice Teachers and Students*, London: Central Council for Education and Training in Social Work and Open Learning Foundation. (Chapter 17)

CCETSW (1995), *Review of the Diploma in Social Work*, Paper 30, London: Central Council for Education and Training in Social Work. (Chapters 13 and 20)

CCETSW (forthcoming, 1995) *Review of the Practice Teaching Award*, Paper 26.4, London: Central Council for Education and Training in Social Work. (Chapter 22)

Collinson, D.L. (1988), *Barriers to Fair Selection*, London: HMSO. (Chapter 7)

Coombe, Vivienne and Little, Alan (1986), *Race and Social Work: A guide to training*, London: Routledge. (Chapter 8)

Coulshed, Veronica (1991), *Social Work Practice* (2nd edn), Houndmills, Basingstoke: British Association of Social Workers/Macmillan. (Chapter 15)

Cross, Terry et al. (1989), *Towards a Culturally Competent System of Care*, CASSP Technical Assistance Center, Washington DC 20007. (Chapter 9)

Cunningham, Ian (1987), 'Openness and Learning to Learn', in Hodgson, Vivien E., Mann, Sarah J. and Snell, Robin (eds), *Beyond Distance Teaching – Towards Open Learning*, Buckingham: Open University Press: 40–58. (Chapter 12)

Curnock, Kathleen and Hardiker, Pauline (1979), *Towards Practice Theory: Skills and Methods in Social Assessments*, London: Routledge and Kegan Paul. (Chapter 15)

Curnock, Kathleen and Prins, Herschel (1982), 'An Approach to Fieldwork Assessment', *British Journal of Social Work*, 12 (5): 507–32. (Chapter 20)

Devore, Wynetta and Schlesinger, Elfriede G. (1991), *Ethnic-Sensitive Social Work Practice* (3rd edn), New York: Macmillan. (Chapter 8)

Doel, Mark (1987a), 'Putting the "Final" in the Final Report', *Social Work Today*, 18 (22): 13. (Chapter 18)

Doel, Mark (1987b), 'The Practice Curriculum', *Social Work Education*, 6 (3): 6–9. (Chapters 5 and 13)

Doel, Mark (1988), 'A Practice Curriculum to Promote Accelerated Learning', in Phillipson, J., Richards, M. and Sawdon, D. (eds), *Towards a Practice-Led Curriculum*, London: National Institute for Social Work: 45–60. (Chapters 13 and 17)

Doel, Mark (1990), 'Putting Heart into the Curriculum', *Community Care*, 797: 20–2. (Chapter 13)

Doel, Mark and Marsh, Peter (1992), *Task-Centred Social Work*, Aldershot: Ashgate. (Chapter 15)

Doel, Mark and Shardlow, Steven (1989), *The Practice Portfolio: A research report*, Department of Sociological Studies, University of Sheffield. (Chapters 18, 19, 20 and 21)

Doel, Mark and Shardlow, Steven (1993), *Social Work Practice: Exercises and activities for training and developing social workers*, Aldershot: Gower. (Chapters 3, 6, 14, 15, 16, 19 and 20)

Doel, Mark and Shardlow, Steven (1995), *Preparing Post-Qualifying Portfolios: A practical guide for candidates*, London: Central Council for Education and Training in Social Work. (Chapter 22)

Dominelli, Lena (1988), *Anti-Racist Social Work*, London: Macmillan. (Chapter 8)

Elgin, Suzette Haden (1989), *Success with the Gentle Art of Verbal Self-Defense*, Englewood Cliffs, NJ: Prentice-Hall. (Chapter 10)

Evans, Dave (1987), 'Live Supervision in the Same Room: A practice teaching method', *Social Work Education*, 6 (3): 13–17. (Chapters 11, 17 and 18)

Evans, Dave (1992), *Assessing Students' Competence to Practise in College and Practice Agency*, London: Central Council for Education and Training in Social Work (first published 1990). (Chapters 15, 19, 20 and 21)

Fisher, Mike, Marsh, Peter and Phillips, David (1986), *In and Out of Care*, London: Batsford. (Chapter 3)

Ford, Kathy and Jones, Alan (1987), *Student Supervision*, Houndmills, Basingstoke: British Association of Social Workers/Macmillan. (Chapters 6 and 16)

Gardiner, Derek (1989), *The Anatomy of Supervision*, Milton Keynes: The Society for Research into Higher Education and The Open University Press. (Chapters 5, 11, 16 and 19)

Haines, John (1985), 'Alternative Frameworks for Organizing the Social Work Syllabus', in Harris, Robert J. et al. (eds), *Educating Social Workers*, Leicester: Association of Teachers in Social Work Education. (Chapter 14)

Hanvey, Chris and Philpot, Terry (1994), *Practising Social Work*, London: Tavistock. (Chapter 15)

Hayward, Christine (1979), *A Fair Assessment: Issues in evaluating coursework*, CCETSW Study No. 2, London: Central Council for Education and Training in Social Work. (Chapter 21)

Honey, Peter and Mumford, Alan (1986), *Manual of Learning Styles*, London: P. Honey. (Chapter 11)

Humphries, Beth, Pankhania-Wimmer, Harsa, Seale, Alex and Stokes, Idris (1993), *Anti-Racist Social Work Education*, Improving Practice Teaching and Learning No. 7, Leeds: Northern Curriculum Development Project and Central Council for Education and Training in Social Work. (Chapter 8)

Knowles, Malcolm (1983), 'Adrogogy: An emerging technology for adult learning', in Tight, Malcolm (ed.), *Adult Learning and Education*: Beckenham: Croom Helm in association with The Open University: 53–71. (Chapter 11)

Kolb, D.A. (1984), *Experiential Learning: Experience as the Source of Learning and Development*, Englewood Cliffs, NJ: Prentice-Hall. (Chapter 15)

Lishman, Joyce (1991), *Handbook of Theory for Practice Teachers in Social Work*, London: Jessica Kingsley. (Chapter 15)

Marsh, Peter and Bayley, Michael (eds) (1984), *Social Skills and Social Work*, Sheffield: Joint Unit for Social Services Research, Sheffield University TV. (Chapter 20)

Marsh, Peter and Triseliotis, John (1992), *Readiness to Practice: Research proposal for the Department of Health and the Scottish Office*, Universities of Sheffield and Edinburgh. (Chapter 21)

Megginson, David and Boydell, Tom (1979), *A Manager's Guide to Coaching*, London: British Association for Commercial and Industrial Education. (Chapter 12)

Morrell, Eric (1979), 'A Lesson in Assessment', *Community Care*, 1 November: 26–8. (Chapter 20)

Payne, Chris and Scott, Terry (1982), *Developing Supervision of Teams in Field and Residential Social Work*, Paper No. 12, London: National Institute for Social Work. (Chapter 16)

Payne, Malcolm (1991), *Modern Social Work Theory: A critical introduction*, Houndmills, Basingstoke: Macmillan. (Chapter 15)

Phillipson, Julia, Richards, Margaret and Sawdon, David (eds) (1988), *Towards a Practice-Led Curriculum*, London: National Institute for Social Work. (Chapter 14)

Richards, Margaret (1988), 'Developing the Content of Practice Teaching (Parts 1 and 2)', in Phillipson, J., Richards, M. and Sawdon, D. (eds), *Towards a Practice-Led Curriculum*, London: National Institute for Social Work: 9–16 and 69–75. (Chapters 13 and 14)

Rojek, Chris, Peacock, Geraldine and Collins, Stewart (1988), *Social Work and Received Ideas*, London: Routledge: Chapter 3. (Chapter 15)

Rowntree, Derek (1991), *Teach Yourself with Open Learning*, Guernsey: Sphere Books. (Chapter 12)

Sawdon, Catherine (1985), 'Action Techniques', printed handout. (Chapters 16 and 20)

Sawdon, David (1986), *Making Connections in Practice Teaching*, London: National Institute for Social Work. (Chapter 14)

Sawdon, David and Sawdon, Catherine (1988), 'Competence and Curriculum – The Practice Teaching Contribution', in Phillipson, J., Richards, M. and Sawdon, D. (eds), *Towards a Practice-Led Curriculum*, London: National Institute for Social Work: 75–9. (Chapters 16 and 19)

Senge, Peter (1990), *The Fifth Discipline: The art and practice of the learning organization*, New York: Doubleday/Currency. (Chapters 12 and 18)

Shakeshaft, Charol (1990), *Gender and Supervision*, Presentation at the Equal Advances in Education Management Conference, December 1990. (Chapter 21)

Shardlow, Steven (1988), *Basic Skills for Practice Teachers*, video, Sheffield: University of Sheffield TV. (Chapters 10 and 18)

Shardlow, Steven (1989a), 'Training and Practice: A fantasy', *Social Work Today*, 20 (20): 36. (Chapter 18)

Shardlow, Steven (1989b), 'The Use of Pre-recorded Video in a Course for Practice Teachers', *Social Work Education*, 8 (2): 25–32. (Chapter 18)

Shardlow, Steven and Doel, Mark (1988), *Placement Triggers*, video, Sheffield: University of Sheffield TV. (Chapter 18)

Shardlow, Steven and Doel, Mark (1993a), 'Towards Anti-Racist Practice Teaching', *Practice*, 6 (3): 219–225. (Chapter 8)

Shardlow, Steven and Doel, Mark (1993b), 'Examination by Triangulation', *Social Work Education*, 12 (3): 67–79. (Chapters 3 and 21)

Shennan, Guy (1995), 'The Student Speaks', unpublished Practice Teaching Portfolio project, Sheffield: Joint Centre. (Chapter 3)

Snell, Robin (1987), 'The Challenge of Painful and Unpleasant Emotions', in Hodgson, Vivien E., Mann, Sarah J. and Snell, Robin (eds), *Beyond Distance Teaching – Towards Open Learning*, Buckingham: Open University Press: 59–71. (Chapter 12)

South Yorkshire (1993), *Practice One Handbook*, Sheffield: South Yorkshire Diploma in Social Work Programme. (Chapters 13, 14, 15, 17, 20 and 21)

Syson, Lucy and Baginsky, M. (1981), *Learning to Practise*, CCETSW Study 3, London: Central Council for Education and Training in Social Work. (Chapter 20)

Thompson, Neil (1993), *Anti-Discriminatory Practice*, Basingstoke: Macmillan. (Chapters 7, 8 and 9)

Williamson, H., Jefferson, R., Johnson, S. and Shabbaz, A. (1989), *Assessment of Practice – A perennial concern?*, Cardiff: University of Wales Social Research Unit. (Chapter 20)

Suggested core texts

It is difficult to recommend 'key texts', and we justify mentioning the following books with the knowledge that the preceding Bibliography is likely to be unmanageable for most busy practitioners.

These are neither standard nor obligatory texts, and they might not be everyone's pick of the bunch. They are noted with the intention of helping you make some early choices about what to read to help support your practice teaching.

Chapters 1–6

Shardlow, Steven and Doel, Mark (1996), *Practice Learning and Teaching*, Houndmills, Basingstoke: Macmillan.

This text is designed for both students and practice teachers. It provides an overview of the theory and practice of student learning on placement.

Butler, Barbara and Elliott, Doreen (1985), *Teaching and Learning for Practice*, Community Care Practice Handbooks, Aldershot: Gower. (100 pp)

Butler and Elliott's book gives a useful overall introduction.

Chapters 7–9

Devore, Wynetta and Schlesinger, Elfriede (1991), *Ethnic-Sensitive Social Work Practice* (3rd edn), New York: Macmillan. (367 pp)

Although its context is North American and it is not specifically written with practice teachers in mind, you will find this book very readable and useful in your work as a practice teacher.

Humphries, Beth, Pankhania-Wimmer, Harsa, Seale, Alex and Stokes, Idris (1993), *Anti-Racist Social Work Education*, Improving Practice Teaching and Learning No. 7, Leeds: Central Council for Education and Training in Social Work. (96 pp)

This is specifically written as a training pack for practice teachers and students. It has a very practical application, with case studies, exercises and activities in a variety of settings.

Thompson, Neil (1993), *Anti-Discriminatory Practice*, Basingstoke: Macmillan. (179 pp)

Doesn't address practice teachers specifically, but gives a very useful and readable synopsis of the current issues. Thompson presents a clear and relatively simple theoretical framework and has especially good chapters on ageism and disability.

Chapters 10–12

Gardiner, Derek (1989), *The Anatomy of Supervision*, Milton Keynes: The Society for Research into Higher Education and The Open University Press. (164 pp)

Much of the adult learning literature is written by educationalists for educationalists, so it is refreshing to have Gardiner's book, which focuses specifically on student supervision in social work and draws from research into adult learning.

Chapters 13–18

Doel, Mark and Shardlow, Steven (1993), *Social Work Practice: Exercises and activities for training and developing social workers*, Aldershot: Gower. (194 pp)

Specifically written for practice teachers as a companion to this book, *Social Work Practice* uses the framework of a Practice Curriculum for a general placement in social work, with activities to trigger the student's learning in each of twenty areas of practice.

Phillipson, Julia, Richards, Margaret and Sawdon, David (eds) (1988), *Towards a Practice-Led Curriculum*, London: National Institute for Social Work. (84 pp)

A collection of articles relating to curriculum issues and very pertinent to practice teaching. This book provides a good introduction to the practice curriculum.

Chapters 19–21

Evans, Dave (reprinted 1992), *Assessing Students' Competence to Practise in College and Practice Agency*, London: Central Council for Education and Training in Social Work. (100 pp)

This is No. 3 in CCETSW's Improving Social Work Education and Training series. It provides a good review of the issues in social work assessment, including methods of gaining information to make assessment judgements and a report of a study on students' views on assessment.

About the authors

Mark Doel is Lecturer in Social Work Studies and Co-Director of the Diploma/MA in Practice Teaching at the University of Sheffield. His work as an independent training consultant takes him far and wide, recently to Moscow and Armenia to help Russian social workers to make training videos. He is currently developing post-qualifying training programmes in groupwork and in task-centred social work.

Steven Shardlow is Senior Lecturer in Social Work Studies, Associate Director of the MA/Diploma in Applied Social Studies and Co-Director of the Diploma/MA in Practice Teaching at the University of Sheffield. Since 1989 he has been the Chairperson of the Association of Teachers in Social Work Education, and he is joint editor of the journal *Issues in Social Work Education*.

Catherine Sawdon is an independent training consultant and has been a Training Officer with a number of agencies, most recently Wakefield Community and Social Services Department. In addition to practice teaching, her interests include anti-oppressive practice, groupwork, staff supervision and counselling. She is a former Chairperson of the National Organisation for Practice Teaching.

David Sawdon has been an independent training consultant since 1989. He has previous experience of social and community work in voluntary and statutory sectors and of university teaching spanning 35 years. He has written widely on practice teaching and staff supervision, often in collaboration with Catherine Sawdon. He is currently book review editor of *Social Work Education*.

By the same authors

Doel, M. and Shardlow, S.M. (1993), *Social Work Practice*, Aldershot: Gower.

Doel, M. and Shardlow, S.M. (eds) (1996), *An International Perspective on Practice Learning*, Aldershot: Arena.

Sawdon, D.T. (1986), *Making Connections in Practice Teaching*, London: National Institute for Social Work.

Shardlow, S.M. and Doel, M. (1996), *Practice Learning and Teaching*, Houndmills, Basingstoke: Macmillan.